BLESSINGS
Through the
WORD

A Journey Toward Spiritual Maturity

Dr. R. J. Lightsey and Rev. Sharen K. Lightsey

Blessings
Through the
Word

*A Journey Toward
Spiritual Maturity*

XULON PRESS

Xulon Press
2301 Lucien Way #415
Maitland, FL 32751
407.339.4217
www.xulonpress.com

© 2021 by Dr. R. J. Lightsey and Rev. Sharen K. Lightsey

All rights reserved solely by the author. The author guarantees all contents are original and do not infringe upon the legal rights of any other person or work. No part of this book may be reproduced in any form without the permission of the author. The views expressed in this book are not necessarily those of the publisher.

Due to the changing nature of the Internet, if there are any web addresses, links, or URLs included in this manuscript, these may have been altered and may no longer be accessible. The views and opinions shared in this book belong solely to the author and do not necessarily reflect those of the publisher. The publisher therefore disclaims responsibility for the views or opinions expressed within the work.

Unless otherwise indicated, Scripture quotations taken from the King James Version (KJV) – *public domain.*

Scripture quotations taken from the Amplified Bible (AMP). Copyright © 1954, 1958, 1962, 1964, 1965, 1987 by The Lockman Foundation. Used by permission. All rights reserved.

Scripture quotations taken from the Holy Bible, New Living Translation (NLT). Copyright ©1996, 2004, 2007 by Tyndale House Foundation. Used by permission of Tyndale House Publishers, Inc.

Scripture quotations taken from the Holy Bible, New International Version (NIV). Copyright © 1973, 1978, 1984, 2011 by Biblica, Inc.™. Used by permission. All rights reserved.

Printed in the United States of America

Paperback ISBN-13: 978-1-66283-418-9
Ebook ISBN-13: 978-1-66283-419-6

Table Of Contents

The Best Is Yet To Come.........................1
Blessed All The Time............................3
Daily Self-Denial..................................6
How Deep Is Your Passion?......................9
God's Ever-Effective Word.................... 13
The Good Fight 15
Listen Closely!................................. 18
The Opportunity To Do Good................. 21
Now! 24
Have You Lost Your Mind? 28
A Love That Gives 30
The Authority Of Jesus........................ 32
It's All Good.................................... 35
Don't Hide Your Light 37
The Throne Of Grace.......................... 39
The Peace God Gives 41
You Make The Choice.......................... 44
The Accuser 46
Walk Worthy................................... 49
How Great Is Our God!........................ 51
Rooted And Grounded In Love................ 54
Why Do I Feel Down?.......................... 56
Feed Us And Fill Us............................ 59
Celebrate Jesus................................ 63
Do You Hear The Words Coming
   Out Of Your Mouth?....................... 65

GRATEFUL EXPECTATION	68
DON'T REJECT THE SON	70
GOD'S NEVER-ENDING PROVISION	73
MAKE PRAYER YOUR PRACTICE	76
EVERYONE IS INCLUDED!	80
LOOK FOR THE GOOD	83
GOD IS OUR REFUGE	85
REMEMBER YOUR SOURCE	88
CAST YOUR CARE	90
THE POWER OF INTERCESSORY PRAYER	92
WALK WORTHY	95
NO CONDEMNATION	98
IT STARTS WITH THE MIND	101
ENDURANCE FOR THE CROWN	104
COMMANDED PROVISION	108
THE RIGHT WAY	112
WHAT IS YOUR FAITH PRODUCING?	114
TAKE OFF THE VEIL	117
HOW TO LIVE AN EFFECTIVE CHRISTIAN LIFE	120
ARE YOU IN?	122
ARE YOU IN? PART 2	125
SUFFICIENCY AND SATISFACTION	127
GOOD NEWS AND HAPPINESS	130
GLORIFY GOD IN YOUR DECISIONS	132

THE BEST IS YET TO COME

> **Proverbs 4:18**
> *But the path of the righteous is like the light of dawn, shining ever brighter until full daylight.*

Path – a way of life, conduct, or thought. It is a course of action, conduct or procedure.

As I was meditating a few weeks ago, I came across this passage of scripture in Proverbs – again. But this time, the words hit me in a different way, and I started thinking about this verse. Scripture encourages believers to live a certain way in this world. We are reminded that we are in the world, but not of the world. This means that though we exist in a place, we do not attach ourselves to our surroundings. We receive our instructions and our direction from someplace else – which implies there is a someplace else somewhere in the universe. Once we are saved our quest is to attach ourselves to this other place that also exists but is one in which we do not see with our physical eyes.

Believers look to scripture to seek instruction and guidance on how we should conduct ourselves while in this world, yet not of this world. This scripture tells us that the path of the righteous is a way of life. It is a specific thought or action, specific conduct or procedure that believers follow. This path is described as the light of dawn, shining brighter and brighter until full daylight. Think about that. The path that we're on gets better and better. It doesn't get worse.

Sometimes we get discouraged along the way. We wonder why things happen to us the way they do when we set ourselves to follow this path and live this life. Why so many disappointments? Why do we personally experience so much wrongdoing aimed against us when we are doing the right and good things?

This scripture is one that ignores the disappointments, setbacks, unfairness & wrongdoings done to us. This scripture wants us to focus on what's ahead. It wants us to focus on the outcome of this way of life. It reminds us that as we continue on this path, things **are** getting better for us. Things are getting brighter. There's something good and amazing that will meet us at the end of our journey in this place.

So, as we set our minds and hearts to live this life, this path, let us encourage ourselves along the way that regardless of what we face, the trials we go through, the questions we may have, the best is yet to come!

BLESSED ALL THE TIME

> *"And it shall come to pass, if thou shalt hearken diligently unto the voice of the Lord thy God, to observe and to do all his commandments which I command thee this day, that the Lord thy God will set thee on high above all nations of the earth: And all these blessings shall come on thee, and overtake thee, if thou shalt hearken unto the voice of the Lord thy God. Blessed shalt thou be in the city, and blessed shalt thou be in the field. Blessed shall be the fruit of thy body, and the fruit of thy ground, the increase of thy kine, and the flocks of thy sheep. Blessed shall be thy basket and thy store. Blessed shall thou be when thou comest in, and blessed shalt thou be when thou goest out"* (Deuteronomy 28:1-6).

What a powerful and dynamic passage of scripture! Moses wrote this book between 1410 B.C and 1406 B.C. In the book of Deuteronomy the Israelites are preparing to enter Canaan and God is giving them instruction on what to expect upon entering the "Promised Land."

There are two (2) things God is instructing the children of Israel to do if they want to be on the receiving end of His all the time blessing: 1) listen to His voice, and 2) keep all His commandments. If they do these two things, God promises to set them high above all nations, bless them in the city, bless them in the field, bless their offspring (descendants), bless what they plant, increase their kine (cows) and increase their sheep. They will always have plenty on hand and stored up for future use. They will be highly blessed when they travel to and from the city. Oh, what a blessing!

As I studied this passage of scripture I became overwhelmed by the promise to bless them all the time and in all areas of their lives. I immediately began to thank God for the blessings I realize and possess each and every day. I'm reminded that all I need God has already provided. I'm reminded that my God delights in blessing me. I'm reminded that I am blessed to be a blessing to others. I am delighted to live the life I love and love the life I live in Christ Jesus. Yet I am still encouraged to daily thank God for who I am (a child of the Most-High King) and why I exist (to bring glory and honor to His Name by letting my light shine).

So here is what is most important. Please do not miss this. I don't live to run or chase after the blessings. If I love God enough to always hear His voice and keep His word the blessings will automatically *"come on me and overtake me" (Deuteronomy 28:2).* The blessings are outstanding and incredible results of love and obedience. My desire is to always hear and obey my God. His promise is to keep me blessed all the time. I confess, I admit – I'm living a blessed life! How about you?

DAILY SELF-DENIAL

Matthew 16:21-26

Obtaining salvation is an event – living a saved life is a process. Too often we see salvation as a one-time event and then it's over. Not so. There is a standard every believer must abide by if he intends to serve and love God with all his heart, mind and soul. Your daily walk is not reduced to simply remembering the day and place you received salvation. But after the receiving, there is a daily commitment to live a life that's pleasing to God. Herein, lies the difficulty and the challenge.

Christ has given us the charge of practicing daily self-denial if in fact we are to continue following Him. Matthew 16:24-26 reads,

> *"If any man will come after me, let him deny himself, take up his cross, and follow me. For whosoever will save his life shall lose it: and whosoever will lose his life for my sake shall find it. For what is a man profited, if he shall gain the whole world, and lose his own soul? Or what shall a man give in exchange for his soul?"*

Daily Self-denial

To "deny" yourself means to refuse your own claims upon yourself. To "take-up" means to lift up – to lift up Jesus (even in times of burden and despair) for all to see. Remember, Jesus said, ***"And I, if I be lifted up from the earth, will draw all men unto me. (John 12:32).*** Christ was lifted up from the ground while on the cross for all to see His suffering death. You and I must lift Him up daily by bearing our crosses and burdens as we follow Him. In doing so, we present Him as the Risen Savior for the world to see.

You must be willing to spiritually kill your flesh every day to deny what you want and what you lay claim to in your life. You must be willing to daily take up your cross and say to the Lord, *"I'll do what makes you happy. Have Thine own way, not my will but Your will be done."*

Jesus commanded Satan to get behind Him (Matthew 16:23) because he did not desire and cherish the things of God nor did he see things from God's point of view. When you follow the Master, you see what He sees. The more you see what He sees the more you follow Him because He orders your steps as you go. The steps of a righteous man are ordered (directed) by the Lord.

Have you "died through self-denial" today? Do you continue to follow God by refusing your own claims on your life? Do you daily remind yourself of your commitment by saying, *"I am not my own. I've been bought with a price and that price is the precious redeeming blood of Jesus?"*

Denying yourself doesn't mean giving up God's blessings and favor. Quite the contrary, it means following Him so all His blessings and favor will follow you and overtake you. God rewards those who seek and follow Him (Hebrews 11:6). You don't get paid first, you follow first! If you want to get what God's got you've got to go where God's going. Deny yourself today and every day and present Christ to the world.

How Deep is Your Passion?

Psalms 119:130-131

One of the things I often wonder about is how much do those of us who say we are followers of Christ love Him? How much do we love His Word? How much do we desire to fulfill His purposes for our lives? How far are we willing to go for Him? To what degree are we willing to lay down our lives for Him? How far does the bar for our surrender and submission go?

For most of us, our desire to please God and live out His word in our lives is very small. For others it's a little deeper. Then there are those who are completely sold out. They love God more than the air they breathe. They are willing to do whatever it takes to please Him. They long for God's presence. They long to spend time in His Word. Their motto is "for God I'll live, and for God, I'll die." They just want Him. If you evaluated yourself today, and included all your circumstances, how deep is your passion?

In Psalms 119: 130-131, the Psalmist writes these words regarding his desire to know God's intentions: ***"I pant with expectation, longing for your commands."*** This verse challenges me. Do I really want to know God's intentions for my life? Do I really seek after God in this way? What about you?

I believe when we are struggling with some things in our lives, there are moments in the struggle when we cry out to God for deliverance. But when we're in the struggle, do we cry out for Him just because we love Him? Do we still desire Him with purity of heart? Or do we just want out because of our discomfort? God's testimony regarding David was that he was a man after His heart. Here's an example of why God said this. When David was in the wilderness running from Saul, he penned these words:

> *"O God, you are my God; I earnestly search for you. My soul thirsts for you; my whole body longs for you in this parched and weary land where there is no water. I have seen you in your sanctuary and gazed upon your power and glory. Your unfailing love is better than life itself; how I praise you! I will praise you as long as I live, lifting up my hands to you in prayer. You satisfy me more than the richest feast. I will praise you with songs of joy. I lie awake thinking of you, meditating on you through the night. Because you are my helper, I sing for joy in the shadow of your wings. I cling to you; your strong right hand holds me securely." (Psalms 63:1-8)*

How Deep Is Your Passion?

When I read these words, I am awed. In the midst of trying to preserve his life from Saul, David's passion for His God was so deep that he took time aside to write these words. His vow to his God was that he would praise him as along as he lived...with no conditions! David's circumstances didn't matter, he just wanted his God! David understood that he could trust God. This trust developed confidence in God that no matter what, God would see him through. He was totally sold out and unashamed of his God. He loved God with his every breath. Again, in Psalms 27, David writes these words:

> *"Though a mighty army surrounds me, my heart will not be afraid.*
> *Even if I am attacked, I will remain confident. The one thing I ask of the Lord— the thing I seek most—is to live in the house of the Lord all the days of my life, delighting in the Lord's perfections and meditating in his Temple. For he will conceal me there when troubles come; he will hide me in his sanctuary. He will place me out of reach on a high rock." (Psalms 27:3-5)*

Do you have this kind of confidence in your God? After all we know about our God through the Scriptures, why are we not more passionate about Him? What prevents us from giving our all to Him? What hinders us from experiencing the very best that our God desires for us?

I believe the time is now for each of us to make a renewed commitment to our God who loves us beyond what words can express. He wants to come back for a church without spot or blemish. He wants our hearts to be pure. The writer of Hebrews exhorts us with these words.

> *"Therefore, since we are surrounded by such a huge crowd of witnesses to the life of faith, let us strip off every weight that slows us down, especially the sin that so easily trips us up. And let us run with endurance the race God has set before us." (Hebrews 12:1)*

God's Ever-Effective Word

> Isaiah 55:11 "So shall my word be that goeth forth out of my mouth: it shall not return unto me void, but it shall accomplish that which I please, and it shall prosper in the thing whereto I sent it."

Several years ago, a slang became very popular among young and old alike. The simple expression "word" was used to confirm someone was speaking "truth to power." The one-word response was (and is still) used to respond that what is being said is agreeable and true. No doubt the person being responded to felt good that the verbalized expressions were received, accepted, and agreed with.

The God of all creation tells us in Isaiah 55:11 that His Word is ever so powerful. "So shall my word be that goeth out of my mouth: it shall not return unto me void, but it shall accomplish that which I please, and it shall prosper in the thing whereto I sent it." What He says and commands will not only definitely come to pass but it will produce His desired result each and every time. The result will always, always return "mission accomplished!" In addition, God's Word will always prosper in every situation and occasion.

Blessings Through the Word

The Merriam-Webster Dictionary defines "prosper" as to become strong and flourishing, to cause to succeed or thrive.

Any way you look at it God's Word improves the situation, circumstance, or person it attaches to. We read these words in 2 Timothy 2:15: Study to show thyself approved unto God, a workman that needeth not to be ashamed, rightly dividing the word of truth." How powerful is that? If we study God's Word to the point of knowing it and knowing how to use it we can speak "truth to power" no matter what the test, trial, or circumstance. But it is imperative that we know God's Word and truly believe that His Word should be spoken by us just as He speaks it. When we say what God says, His Word goes out and immediately begins to accomplish things and produce positive results. But, we must say what God says – not what man says or what we want to hear.

You may have heard the expression – "If God said it, I believe it, and that settles it." But here is my response to that. "If God said it, that settles it because His Word never returns unto Him void (empty)! Always seek, receive, and act on God's ever-effective Word.

The Good Fight

1 Timothy 1:18-19; 6:12; 2 Timothy 4:7
This charge, son Timothy, I put to you, in keeping with the prophecies already made about you, so that by these prophecies you may fight the good fight, armed with trust and a good conscience. (1 Timothy 1:18-19)
Fight the good fight for the true faith. Hold tightly to the eternal life to which God has called you, which you have declared so well before many witnesses. (1 Timothy 6:12)
I have fought the good fight, I have finished the race, and I have remained faithful. (2 Timothy 4:7)

These words were written by the Apostle Paul to Timothy, his son in the faith. They are letters written from a spiritual father to his spiritual son. When one reads these letters, the reader can not help but notice the very intimate and strong bond between these two men.

In his first letter to Timothy, Paul instructed Timothy on the importance of order in the church. He also encouraged his son to stay strong to the sound teachings he had been instructed in. Apparently, Timothy was facing great opposition from people who were twisting the scriptures. These people had persuasive arguments. They were challenging. They were willfully ignorant of the truth. He instructed him not to get caught up in the arguments of these people, but to keep his focus and pursue godliness as his way of life.

Timothy was in a fight. He was in a struggle. This fight was taking a lot out of him. But Paul wrote to encourage and remind him about the things he had been taught so he would gain strength to keep fighting the good fight of the faith.

In his second letter to his son, Paul continued to encourage Timothy. He told him to not be ashamed to tell others about the Lord, and to not shrink away from the suffering, or of him who was in prison. He reminded Timothy that he was also in the same fight. That it was because of the gospel that he was in prison. But he told Timothy that he was okay with it because he understood that those who live godly in Christ will suffer persecution. He encouraged him to endure the sufferings along with him. He told him to fight the good fight.

Paul instructed Timothy to stay in companionship with those who also believed in the Lord, Jesus. And he reminded him again to not get involved with those who wanted to argue and start fights. He told him that evil people would flourish and get worse and worse.

The Good Fight

Then Paul told Timothy that he himself had fought the good fight. He had finished his race, and he had remained faithful. Consequently, he knew he had a reward – a crown of righteousness which the Lord was going to give Him on the day of his return. But not for him only, but for all those who love his appearing. (2 Timothy 4:8)

My brothers and sisters, we, too must fight the good fight of the faith. Sometimes the fight is hard, but we must remember these words of encouragement that Paul wrote to Timothy. We must keep in mind that each of us has his/her own race to run. No matter what comes our way, we must stay true to God, and to sound doctrine. Yes, things are going to get worse and worse. But regardless of the struggle, we must do the work of an evangelist, and be faithful to our Lord. We must fight the good fight.

Listen Closely!

1 Kings 19

In 1 Kings 19, we read the account of the prophet Elijah running in fear for his life. The queen Jezebel had placed a hit on him after he had killed the 400 prophets of Baal. He journeyed about eighty miles from Samaria before he actually slowed down a little. He rested under a juniper tree and asked the Lord to let him die. He had given up. All his zeal had left him. He went to sleep and an angel woke him up and told him to eat. He ate and fell asleep again. The angel woke him a second time and told him to eat some more because the journey was too great for him. The food that Elijah ate kept him for 40 days and 40 nights!

While Elijah continued on his journey he came to a cave and the Word of God came to him and asked him what he was doing. He responded that he had been very jealous for the Lord, the Israelites had forsaken His covenant, thrown down His altars, and killed the prophets. And he added he was the only one left, and now his life was on the line. (1 Kings 19: 9-10) God told him to leave the cave and stand on the mountain.

As Elijah was standing on the mountain, the Lord passed by, and a great and strong wind tore through the mountains and broke in pieces the rocks, but the Lord was not in the earthquake. Then a fire came, but the Lord was not in the fire. After the fire…listen closely…there was a **sound** of gentle stillness, **and** a still, small voice. (1 Kings19:12) Notice what Elijah did after he heard the **sound** of this still small voice. He hid his face in the mantle and stood in the entrance of the cave. Then the voice asked the same question as he heard earlier. "What are you doing here, Elijah"? Elijah gave the same response as he did earlier as well. (v. 10)

At this moment Elijah and God began to have a conversation – a two-way conversation. Elijah was now in a position to not only state his grievance, but to **listen** to what God wanted to say to him about his situation.

You see, I believe, it's not that believers don't pray to God. The problem is that we don't wait long enough to **hear** from God. We state our case, we list our grievances, and we walk away feeling as if God hasn't heard us. It's not that God doesn't hear us. We don't hear Him! We are the ones who are not listening! We are the ones who are so wrapped up in what's happening to us, that we don't take the required time to hear from the One who is listening to us. We need to listen closely! We need to slow down, and wait for God to speak. He's not always where there is the most noise. Sometimes He's in the very quiet.

We may be looking for God in the wrong place, when all He wants from us is to be still and listen closely. When Elijah finally allowed himself to hear from God, he found that things were not as bad as he believed they were. God let him know that there were going to be some political changes – He was going to anoint a new king in Syria, and Jehu was going to take over the throne in Israel (which let

Blessings Through the Word

him know that Jezebel was not an issue for him). There was also going to be a change in the spiritual leadership. Elisha was going to take over his position as prophet. Then the Lord gave Elijah some comfort. He told him that he wasn't the only one who was left, there were seven thousand in Israel that had not bowed down to Baal! Seven thousand!

The work that Elijah had done in Israel, his prophetic words, did have some impact! There were some who heard the Word of the Lord and believed! He did have some results! It wasn't all for nothing! What a feeling of comfort Elijah had in this knowledge...and all because he slowed down enough to listen!

My brothers and sisters, this is a very important lesson for us to put into action. Take the time to hear God's voice. He does care. He is concerned. He has a plan. We just need to listen closely!

The Opportunity to Do Good

Galatians 6:9-10
"And let us not be weary in well doing: for in due season we shall reap, if we faint not. As we have therefore opportunity, let us do good unto all me, especially unto them who are of the household of faith" (KJV).

As a Chaplain for Tyson Foods, I had the opportunity to serve on one of several disaster relief teams dispatched to eastern North Carolina to assist and comfort those affected by Hurricane Florence last month. Food and water were freely supplied and donated by Tyson Foods to all who needed assistance. Over 250,000 meals were prepared and some delivered with the help of local volunteers and the National Guard. It is an honor and a privilege to be associated with a company that would do so much for those in need – not only as a result of Hurricane Florence, but whenever there is a major disaster anywhere in the country.

This (and other acts of unselfish kindness) reminds me of what Paul stated in his letter to the church at Galatia.

"As we have therefore opportunity, let us do good unto all men, especially unto them who are of the household of faith" (Galatians 6:10). He instructed them to not only look for and recognize opportunities to help others, but to go beyond and to actually ***"do good unto them."*** What does this mean for us? This act requires being attentive to the needs and concerns of others, determining what we have and what we can do to assist them in their time(s) of need, and then taking action. Paul went further in his directive to the Galatians by stating they should ***"especially do good unto those who are of the household of faith."*** Who are those described as being in the "household of faith?" Ephesians 2:19 describes them as ***fellowcitizens with the saints***, those who are of the household of God – simply put, born again believers should receive first priority!

Certainly the question will (and often does) arise, "What if they really don't need my help? What if they are scheming and plotting to get something for nothing? What if they are trying to take advantage of me?" First of all, let's admit we all want to sow our seed in good ground. We don't want what we give to be wasted, misused or unappreciated. But there are two important points I want to make. First, we should allow the Holy Spirit to lead and guide us in each and every situation. No doubt there have been and will continue to be times when we know those asking or seeking help really don't need it or have misused it on every previous occasion. The Holy Spirit gives us wisdom. He leads and guides us. In addition, the longer we dwell on those questions and try to rationalize who we help, the longer the needed remains in need. We have two (2) commands: 1) Recognize the opportunity, and 2) Do good.

The Opportunity To Do Good

We have been blessed to be a blessing. Oftentimes, what we give to others can be the ministry of presence (being there for and with them without providing money or other tangible items). Taking time to pray is another way of doing good for others. May we consistently seek and take advantage of the opportunity to do good.

Now!

The definition of the word now is "at the present time or moment". It does not refer to future events or feelings. It is present. The problem that humans have is that we often live our lives looking for and/or expecting something to happen, or looking back at something in the past. For whatever reason, focusing on the now or the present is a challenge. But faith works in the present, not in the future. Faith is now! We might receive what we want at some point in the future, but we live and think and operate as though we have it now!

Believers must learn to live in the present knowing that all of God's promises are ours now! However, the manifestation of some of those promises won't be fully awarded to us until the appointed time. Unfortunately, some believers focus so much on their past behaviors and choices before they fully committed to Christ, that they don't understand where they are now.

The word of God reminds us of the importance of now. Let's look at a few scriptures.

> *But <u>now</u> you have been united with Christ Jesus. Once you were far away*

> *from God, but <u>now</u> you have been brought near to him through the blood of Christ. (Eph. 2:11-13).*

Paul is reminding the believers at Ephesus that they should keep in mind where they've come from. He's not implying that they should focus on their past condition, but while focusing on their present condition in Christ, they should be mindful of how much Christ has done for them and where they are now.

> *Because of Christ and our faith in him, we can <u>now</u> come boldly and confidently into God's presence. (Eph. 3:12).*

Again, Paul is reminding the believers at Ephesus that things have changed. Our faith has changed our position from being on the outside and apart from God, to being on the inside. We have sonship authority that allows us to boldly and confidently come into the Father's presence. We have this authority now!

> *And <u>now</u> that you belong to Christ, you are the true children of Abraham. You are his heirs, and God's promise to Abraham belongs to you. (Gal 3:29).*

Now that we belong to Christ by faith, we are also connected to Abraham, and are positioned to receive whatever promise God made to Abraham. The promise is ours now! Paul tells the Corinthians that God has commissioned us and enables us to stand firm in Christ. God has identified us by placing the Holy Spirit as the first installment that guarantees everything He has promised us. *(2 Cor. 1:20)*

> *Yet <u>now</u> he has reconciled you to himself through the death of Christ in his physical body. As a result, he has brought you into his own presence, and you are holy and blameless as you stand before him without a single fault. (Col. 1:22).*

Since we have accepted Christ, we are now reconciled to Him because of his physical death. We are now in His presence, and he sees us as not having any fault. This is where are now! This is how God sees us now! He sees us with pure love with no faults, no issues, no shortcomings, no sin! We are without fault now!

These are just a few scriptures to remind us that things have changed for us now that we have Christ. His Holy Spirit confirms our position with the Father. He shows His love for us every day we are here because Today is the present time. It is the "now" time. Our success requires us to live in the present. Our miracles are happening now. Our prayers are being answered now. Our expectations are at work now.

When we can focus on now, I believe we will live out the words of Christ when He told the disciples that they would do greater works than He did because He was going back to His Father. What did He mean? I believe part of what He was saying was that as long as we are here on the earth, we are under assignment from God. Consequently, we will see and experience God's power in the earth realm now.

NOW!

When we don't experience the great power of God, it's because we are not following Christ's example. We must think in the present. We must pray now. We must expect now. We must have faith now. When we do, there is no doubt in my mind that Christ's love and power will spread in the earth realm, and we will live lives of victory and have great success.

HAVE YOU LOST YOUR MIND?

> *"And be not conformed to this world: but be ye transformed by the renewing of your mind, that ye may prove what is that good, and acceptable, and perfect, will of God" (Romans 12:2).*
>
> *"Let this mind be in you, which was also in Christ Jesus..." (Philippians 2:5).*

I will get right to the point and ask the question. "Have you lost your mind?" No, I don't mean have you become mentally unstable or out of balance. I want to know have you been born again and placed yourself in position to think like Christ Jesus? In the apostle Paul's letter to the church at Rome he instructs them not to change themselves to be like people of the world but to let God change them inside to a new way of thinking. *"And be not conformed to this world: but be ye transformed by the renewing of your mind, that ye may prove what is that good, and acceptable, and perfect, will of God" (Romans 12:2).* To the Philippian church he wrote, *"Let this mind be in you, which was also in Christ Jesus..." (Philippians 2:5).* In other words, as you strive to operate as one body also strive to think like Christ thought.

Have You Lost Your Mind?

In order to think like Christ, you must *"lose or abolish"* your sinful and worldly mind and replace it with the mind of the Savior. First, of course, you must not only identify with the Savior but you must be in Him. If any man be in Christ, he is a new creation (2 Corinthians 5:17). The new creation comes with a new mind that must be continually programmed with Christ-like data. This Christ-like data is the will of God and the way of God according to the Word of God. You must continually feed your mind with positive thoughts so that foul and negative thoughts don't occupy your thinking and meditative processes.

I recently led a teaching during a married couples fellowship. I informed some and reminded others that it is impossible for your mind to entertain two thoughts at the same moment. Of course you can switch from thinking on one thing and immediately turn your attention to another thought. However, when you do, the initial (first) thought has left and can only return (and remain) when you allow it. So, with the ability to control your thoughts, you can lose your mind to thoughts that are not pleasing to God and let thoughts that are pleasing to Him reside in your thought process.

So many times we hear people say "I want to be more like Christ." I too, strive to be more like Jesus. But we (you and I) must realize that it takes a concentrated and pointed effort to live the way Christ lived here on earth and to think like He thinks. That literally means leaving and dismissing the way the world sees and analyzes things and accepting and admitting the way Christ thinks.

A Love That Gives

> "For God so loved the world that He gave His only begotten Son, that whosoever believeth in Him should not perish, but have everlasting life." (John 3:16, KJV)

We are now in the "holiday" season. More specifically, we are a few weeks away from Christmas – the holiday many people acknowledge and recognize by giving gifts to family and friends. In the worldly tradition, Christmas is synonymous with shopping, grand dinners, office parties, decorations, and time off from work. However, there is a great difference if we approach and celebrate this "holiday" season in recognition of and appreciation for what God did for mankind.

In reference to John 3:16, we see that God "so loved" that He gave all He had for the sole benefit of those who would graciously receive His gift. The word "so" is an adverb and in this context it modifies the past tense verb "loved." It tells us the degree to which God loved us. That degree moved Him to action – not only to give a Gift, but to give a Gift of ultimate sacrifice. God gave all He had. He gave the only Gift that would permit and allow mankind to inherit and forever possess eternal life. If we don't grasp the thought that God gave us exactly what we needed and could not provide for ourselves, we remain lost and empty.

It is by receiving God's Gift that mankind moves from hopelessness to hope and from despair to abundant life. The reward for receiving His Gift is immeasurable and priceless. But yet, and most important of all, the Gift is easily and readily accessible. **We don't have to "shop around," but simply seek first the Kingdom of God and His righteousness and everything we need for sustainability and abundant living will also be ours – all because God loved so much that He gave exactly what we needed (Matthew 6:33).**

As we celebrate the birth of Jesus Christ, (our Lord and Savior), may we present Him to others as the Gift needed to experience happiness, joy, and peace. And as we interact with family and friends through the sharing of material gifts, let's remember (and never forget) to give because of love – not because of expectation, ritual, or tradition. It's all about a love that gives and a gift that is freely received without expecting a "payback gift" in return. There is truth in the saying "love isn't love until you give it away.

THE AUTHORITY OF JESUS

Authority defined by dictionary.com is as follows:

1. The power to determine, adjudicate, or otherwise settle issues or disputes; jurisdiction; the right to control, command, or determine.
2. A power or right delegated or given; authorization; Who has the authority to grant permission?
3. A person or body of persons in whom authority is vested, as a governmental agency.

When you study these definitions of authority, Jesus encompasses all of these. The word authority is a legal term. Throughout Jesus' ministry, He only did what was legal. He never went outside of those bounds. Legally, He could speak and it was done. He could delegate legally which He did when He sent His disciples out to cast out demons and heal sickness.

He made many attempts to help his disciples recognize and understand His authority. He did this through His teachings, through the miracles He performed, even speaking to the natural elements in the earth by calming the wind and the waves, and walking on water. And of course, He proved his authority over death when He was raised

The Authority Of Jesus

from the dead. (Col. 1:18) The scriptures tell us that Jesus has all authority in heaven and in earth. (Mat. 28:18)

One of my favorite examples that bring this to light is the story of the paralyzed man found in both (Matthew 9:1-8 & Mark 2: 1-12). Often in scripture Jesus referred to Himself as the Son of Man. This title demonstrates the authority of Jesus as a human on earth.

Consequently, He showed us how we have the same authority as humans while on earth.

The paralyzed man was healed because of the words Jesus **spoke** to him. When He first told him that his sins were forgiven, He was telling the man that his sins were put away, that there was no more penalty. He was telling him that he was not guilty, and his relationship with God was restored. How do you think the man felt when Jesus spoke these words that legally freed him from feeling the condemnation of sin? Once he accepted Jesus' words of release and forgiveness, he could then accept his healing. The man was no longer legally bound to his sickness. He was now free. At that point, Jesus could instruct him on what do.

The scribes had a problem with Jesus' authority. They didn't understand. They were blind to the legal spiritual laws. So, Jesus asked them which would be easier **to say**? Did you get that? **"to say**."

> *"Is it easier **to say** to the paralyzed man 'Your sins are forgiven,' or 'Stand up, pick up your mat, and walk'? So, I will prove to you that the Son of Man has the authority on earth to forgive sins." Then Jesus turned*

> *to the paralyzed man <u>and said</u>, "Stand up, pick up your mat, and go home!" And the man jumped up, grabbed his mat, and walked out through the stunned onlookers. They were all amazed and praised God, exclaiming, "We've never seen anything like this before!" (Mark 2:9-12)*

This miracle occurred just on Christ using His authority by speaking life to the paralytic man. Paul writes to the Colossian church that Christ is supreme in all things.

> *"Christ is the visible image of the invisible God. He existed before anything was created and is supreme over all creation, for through him God created everything in the heavenly realms and on earth. He made the things we can see and the things we can't see—such as thrones, kingdoms, rulers, and authorities in the unseen world. Everything was created through him and for him. He existed before anything else, and he holds all creation together." (Col. 1:15-17)*

Scripture after scripture attests to Jesus' authority. Once we can truly accept the authority of Jesus, we truly can do all through Christ who strengthens us. (Phil. 4:13).

It's All Good

And God saw everything that he had made, and behold, it was very good" (Genesis 1:31).

The response I give most often when asked how I am doing is, "It's all good." A few moments before beginning to write this devotion someone asked me how I was doing and instantly the response was "It's all good." I took a few moments to think about why I give that response. The reason is that all God has created (including today and every day) is good.

In Genesis 1:1-30 we read several verses that state all that God created was good. In verse 31 we read the conclusion of the whole matter – "And God saw everything that he had made, and behold, it was very good." Notice that His work is described as "very good." There is nothing God has created that was not good or meant for good.

I have often heard people talk about having a bad day. I submit that there are no bad days. Every day the Lord brings into fruition is a "good day." God does not create bad days. Yes, some bad things may happen, but they happen on "good days" because "good days' are the only days God creates. What helps us to get through and remain standing when bad things happen is to remember what God's Word tells us in Psalms 118:24 – "This is the day which the Lord hath made; we will rejoice and be glad in it."

The challenge should ever be to remember and to say it's all good. Not only is God good (all the time) but what He created and brought into fruition, whether tangible or intangible was meant (intended) for our good. I choose to make the best of every situation and I challenge you and all members of the royal family to do the same. Maybe you don't feel well or have been treated unfairly. Maybe your best friend stabbed you in the back. Maybe words can't express the dirt that has been shoveled on you with intended retaliation. Take God's Word and use it for encouragement and to your advantage. Remember what Romans 8:28 tells us – "And we know that all things work together for good to them that love God, to them who are the called according to his purpose."

When you are in the midst of unfortunate situations and circumstances take time to remember that even though some bad things are happening, it's a good day. Say with your mouth and believe in your heart that it's all good!

Don't Hide Your Light

Matthew 5:14-16 "You are the light of the world—like a city on a hilltop that cannot be hidden. No one lights a lamp and then puts it under a basket. Instead, a lamp is placed on a stand, where it gives light to everyone in the house. In the same way, let your good deeds shine out for all to see, so that everyone will praise your heavenly Father.

There are gifts and talents that God has put inside each of us that need to be seen. They are not to be hidden. We need to display what God has put inside of us, not that we want attention for ourselves or to "be seen by men", but so that God will be seen in us. He wants us to show Him to the world. Why? So that men will see His good work in us and give praise to Him. It's really that simple.

As we move into the new year, we should have already been seeking God on what we want for our lives. When the new year comes in, we don't need to start the process of what we desire. We should already be preparing our minds and hearts for the manifestation. What do you want to move into next year? What is holding you back from shining your light?

We should let God be seen in us by letting our light shine in our circles of influence...in our homes, our churches, our places of employment, and in our communities. Remind yourself that God did not give you the gifts you have to be hidden. Let others see your light. Jesus said that "No one lights a lamp and then puts it under a basket. Instead, a lamp is placed on a stand, where it gives light to everyone in the house." (Matthew 5:15).

Don't hide your light! Let those gifts come forth! Don't let others intimidate you and make you feel as if you don't measure up to their standards. Even more, don't put restraints on yourself! Let your light shine! Let those things that God put in you come out of you so that others will see and give glory to Him! Let your light – your gifts, your talents be seen! It's what God wants!

The Throne of Grace

Hebrews 4:14-16
"Seeing then we have a great high priest, that is passed into the heavens, Jesus the Son, let us hold fast our profession. For we have not a high priest which cannot be touched with the feeling of our infirmities; but was in all points tempted like as we are, yet without sin. Let us therefore come boldly to the throne of grace, that we may obtain mercy, and find grace to help in time of need (Hebrews 4:14-16, KJV).

Oftentimes, I enjoy sitting alone in our family room with no sound of the television, music, or other distractions. These moments provide me the time and atmosphere to think on God's goodness and greatness. They also are times when I express my sincere gratitude for Who He is and what He means to me. It's important (at least for me) to have the correct physical setting as I am ushered into the time of spiritual worship.

Hebrews 4:14-16 speaks to me as words of encouragement when I need to enter that "quiet place." This spiritual place is where Christ intercedes for me. Not only does He have access to the Father but He is seated in the very presence of God the Father. But prior to this position, He partook of man's nature and temptations so that He might sympathize and He did so "without sinning."

It is at this place, this spiritual point of connection, this throne of grace, that we find authority and provision. As Christians, born again and blood washed believers we have access to a place (the place) to obtain God's grace whenever we need it. We have a place reserved especially for us to be comforted, instructed, challenged, encouraged and whatever else we need. Isn't it wonderful that God not only loves us unconditionally but also provides a place and the opportunity for us to be refueled and recharged?

With all that has been said, there is something else to be addressed. Verse 16 of Hebrews 4 commands we should "boldly" come to the throne of grace. This means we should come with power and force. We should not have a lazy or defeated attitude when we come to that special spiritual place. Remember, it's one thing to approach the throne but it's something totally different and quite beneficial to come to that spiritual place correctly, that is "boldly" and with expectations of receiving God's grace!

THE PEACE GOD GIVES

> John 14:27
> "I am leaving you with a gift—peace of mind and heart. And the peace I give is a gift the world cannot give. So, don't be troubled or afraid.

As Jesus is preparing His disciples for His departure from earth and His return to His Father in Heaven, He tells them that He's leaving them with a gift of peace. This peace was of a sort that they could not find in the world. It's a gift that comes from another place.

Peace in Hebrew means "shalom". Its full definition means completeness. It means complete peace. It encompasses feelings such as contentment, completeness, wholeness, well-being and harmony. The opposite of peace is to be troubled, agitated, worried, fearful, etc. When one is at peace in mind and heart, then he/she is not impacted by feelings of worry or fear. He/she is not unsettled or feeling anxious.

How does one receive and maintain this kind of peace? The prophet Isaiah wrote "You will keep in perfect peace all who trust in you, all whose thoughts are fixed on you! (Isaiah 26:3). The key to maintaining this gift of peace is to keep your mind and heart fixed on your God! Think about Him, desire Him, yearn for Him, seek Him! Then you won't have those feelings of agitation and anxiety.

Paul wrote these words to the Philippian church "Don't worry about anything; instead, pray about everything. Tell God what you need, and thank him for all he has done. Then you will experience God's peace, which exceeds anything we can understand. His peace will guard your hearts and minds as you live in Christ Jesus. (Phil 4:6-7).

Paul describes the process of peace. First, we should not worry about anything, but instead pray about everything. Second, we should have hearts of gratitude. We need to practice saying "Thank you" to Him for all that He's already done for us. This attitude of thankfulness leads us into peace (shalom). It goes past our understanding, but it's something that is real and is to be experienced by us. The peace that God gives guards or protects our hearts and minds as we live in Christ Jesus! This is exciting! This is powerful! This is how we live in joy!

Paul also encouraged the Thessalonian believers with these words "Now may the Lord of peace himself give you his peace at all times and in every situation. The Lord be with you all". Again, we see that this peace is given to us by God. Paul's prayer for the believers is that the Lord himself gives his peace to us at all times in every situation. Wow! This means that it is possible for us to have peace no matter what our circumstances are! It is a gift that Jesus promised his disciples and a gift that is for the body of Christ. My prayer is that the church of today will live in the peace that God gives!

You Make the Choice

> "All scripture is given by inspiration of God, and is profitable for doctrine, for reproof, for correction, for instruction in righteousness: that the man of God may be perfect, thoroughly furnished unto all good works" 2 Timothy 3:16-17 KJV).

The scripture referenced above is truly one of my favorites. The two verses have always reminded me that whatever man needs to know about life – the purpose, the formula for success, the antidote for all ills, and everything else can be found in the Word of God. These verses tell us that God inspired men of His choice to write His messages of believing, encouraging, chastising, and teaching so that we (His creation) could live the best life possible.

Yet, with that being said, I still converse with people who find a way to bring in their belief that the holy scriptures, the Bible, is merely a collection of history and mankind's guide to "live a good life" and to share his individual thoughts and promote his own agenda. But that is not what concerns me the most. What's most troubling for me is that they don't want me to believe as I do: that all scripture is given by inspiration of God. Yes, God inspired and used man (humans) to record His instruction and direction for all human life. In addition, He let it be known that all of His inspired and written Word is profitable. It is of the utmost value.

My response is never to try to convince them of God's Word through an argument. I simply state that I believe what is written is God inspired just as much (and probably more) as they say otherwise. I encourage all believers to do the same. God's Word is not to be argued over. Our Creator, the Heavenly Father has given each of us the ability and privilege of deciding to accept or reject His Word. Therefore, we should respond to the "naysayers" by simply saying. "You make the choice." Yes, they are free to believe what they want to believe and the best thing we can do is pray for them to come to accept God's Word by faith. We don't need their permission to pray for them so they can't hinder our act of doing so.

I have learned that rather than becoming upset, frustrated, or angry with them to simply listen and allow them to share their thoughts. I share mine and then tell them "you make the choice." I hope this process is of benefit to all believers and "you make the choice" be known as our final statement in the conversation.

THE ACCUSER

Job 1:6-2:1-10

Accuser – Diablos meaning adversary, enemy, or slanderer. It is a legal term used in the context of one bringing a charge against another. Scripture describes Satan in these terms: the accuser of the brethren, adversary, enemy.

Satan, the Accuser, constantly brings charges to God against us. He watches us closely, develops his strategy, and goes in for the kill. We must know not only who we are, but who our enemy is. Not knowing our enemy is where we fail. Our accuser is expert not only in this area, but also in deception. This truth is illustrated in the book of Job.

In Chapters one and two, we find two instances when Satan came to God to accuse Job. "One day the members of the heavenly court came to present themselves before the Lord, and the Accuser, Satan came with them." (Job 1:6)

This is a legal setting. The spirits (angels) of God presented their cases before Him. The heavenly court allows the accuser to present as well. This was the case with Job. In the dialogue between Satan and God, God commends

THE ACCUSER

Job for his integrity and reverence for Him. However, Satan brings forth the accusation that Job only has integrity and reverence because God has faithfully put a wall of protection around him, his home and family. If these were taken away, Job would no longer have reverence for God, and would surely curse him to His face.

Once the accuser presented his accusation against Job, God allowed Job to experience a season of testing giving the accuser an opportunity to win his case. Thus, it was on the accuser to prove his case against Job. God gave him permission to take all of Job's possessions and even took all of his children away. Satan did this in a way that was deceptive. He made it look like God was involved in his loss. For Job's reply was "I came naked from my mother's womb, and I will be naked when I leave. The Lord gave me what I had, and the Lord has taken it away. Praise the name of the Lord! In all of this, Job did not sin by blaming God." (Job 1:20-21)

Still, the accuser was not willing to lose his case against Job, and presented to God another accusation against him. This time, he challenged God with these words. "A man will give up everything he has to save his life. But reach out and take away his health, and he will surely curse you to your face!" (Job 2: 4-5).

God again gave Satan the opportunity to prove his case, and Satan struck Job with painful sores all over his body. Job described it like this: "My body is covered with maggots and scabs. My skin breaks open, oozing with pus." (Job 7:5).
Although Job did not sin by blaming God for his losses or the attack on his health, he thought God was the cause.

"Why won't you leave me alone, at least long enough for me to swallow! If I have sinned, what have I done to you, O watcher of all humanity? Why make me your target? Am I a burden to you? Why not just forgive my sin and take away my guilt? (Job 7:19-20)

The Accuser's goal is to separate us from our Father. He will attempt to do this by any means at his disposal. How do we win? We follow Christ's example of trusting in God's Word. Just as Christ depended on the Word of His Father in His season of testing, we must follow his example when we undergo our seasons of testing. We must know our Father, know His Word, use His Word to win our battles, and acknowledge the power of His Word to make us victorious over the power of our enemy.

WALK WORTHY

> "I therefore, the prisoner of the Lord, beseech you that ye walk worthy of the vocation wherewith ye are called, with all lowliness and meekness, with longsuffering, forbearing one another in love; endeavoring to keep the unity of the Spirit in the bond of peace" (Ephesians 4:1, KJV).

In the fourth chapter of the apostle Paul's writing to the church (believers) at Ephesus around A.D. 60, he addresses their relationships with other believers. He instructs and encourages them to walk worthy of the vocation (lifestyle) they have been instructed to live with others. He challenges them to be unified in the Spirit of peace.

Once we attain and announce the status of being born again believers (through the work of Christ the Anointed One) we have a charge to walk worthy of the new lifestyle we have adopted. In 2 Corinthians 5:17 we read, "Therefore if any man be in Christ, he is a new creature: old things have passed away; behold, all things are become new", KJV). When we make that confession of accepting Christ as Lord and Savior, we commit to living a life that is pleasing to

God. The "old way" of living passes away. The old way may include lying, jealousy, hatred, fornication, gluttony, envy, strife, stealing, and much more. The new way of living graduates or promotes us to truth, honesty, love, faithfulness, meekness, peace, and the like. We are instructed to live this new lifestyle and "walk worthy" of the confession we have made that we are the Lord's representatives.

How we interact, communicate, and treat others will be shown by the walk we project and the sincerity of our commitment. It all centers around maintaining peace with others in our daily walk. Sure there will be days when we are tried or challenged. Sure there will be days of opportunities to overcome and dealing with people who may be trying "our last nerve." But the challenge and directive from the apostle Paul is to walk worthy of who we are and Whose we are. Our light should shine before men that they see our good works and glorify our Father Who is in heaven. We should always represent the kingdom well.

We should be patient and exhibit understanding with others, knowing that the God we serve is able to remedy any situation or circumstance. We should be confident in knowing that all things work together for good to those who love God and are the called according to his purpose. Here is the question. Is your walk a worthy walk?

How Great is Our God!

> This is what the Lord says: "Heaven is my throne, and the earth is my footstool. Could you build me a temple as good as that? Could you build me such a resting place? My hands have made both heaven and earth; they and everything in them are mine. I, the Lord, have spoken!
> (Isaiah 66:1-2)

God Almighty, through the prophet Isaiah tells us that heaven contains the throne of God where He reigns! These verses give us a picture of how great and powerful our God is as He sits on His throne. Just think of how vast heaven must be to occupy the throne of God! A throne is defined as "the chair or seat occupied by a sovereign, bishop, or other exalted personage on ceremonial occasions, usually raised on a dais and covered with a canopy."

On a previous occasion, the prophet described the vision he saw of God's glory. "It was in the year King Uzziah died that I saw the Lord. He was sitting on a lofty throne, and the train of his robe filled the Temple." (Isaiah 6:1). The reaction of the prophet to this heavenly vision was so overwhelming that he literally felt like he would die because he saw himself and his nation as filthy in the presence of God.

God told the prophet that no man-made structure could contain him, because He himself made the heaven and earth and that everything in them were His! Think about that! This is a description of a God Whose power has no limits! The prophet Jeremiah acknowledged this when he said "O Sovereign Lord! You made the heavens and earth by your strong hand and powerful arm. Nothing is too hard for you! (Jeremiah 32:7).

King Solomon, too, acknowledged the greatness of God in his prayer after he had finished building the temple for the Lord's name. "But will God really live on earth among people? Why, even the highest heavens cannot contain you. How much less this Temple I have built! (2 Chronicles 6:18).

Brothers and sisters, it would do us well to keep in mind how great our God is. We must continuously, unceasingly, without stopping acknowledge the greatness of our God. We must live in complete and unwavering confidence in our God at all times – under every circumstance. Jesus Himself taught us this in the model prayer. Our Father in heaven, may your name be kept holy. (Matthew 6:9).

The key word is "kept" which indicates we must hold onto and maintain our view of our God continuously. We must represent Him truthfully by acknowledging our

God's power and glory at all times for our God, indeed, is a great God!

Rooted and Grounded in Love

> "For this cause I bow my knees unto the Father of our Lord Jesus Christ, of Whom the whole family in heaven and earth is named, that he would grant you, according to the riches of his glory, to be strengthened with might by his Spirit in the inner man; that Christ may dwell in your hearts by faith ; that ye, being rooted and grounded in love, may be able to comprehend with all saints what is the breadth, and length, and depth, and height; and to know the love of Christ, which passeth knowledge, that ye might be filled with all the fullness of God (Ephesians 3:14-17, KJV).

In Chapter 3 of Ephesians, the apostle Paul writes to the church at Ephesus and tells the believers that he prays for them. His prayer is that God would grant many things for them. One of his prayer requests is that they would be "rooted and grounded in love," (verse 17). Dictionary.com defines "rooted" as being firmly planted and "grounded" as

Rooted And Grounded In Love

fixed firmly, settled, or established. Thus, his prayer is for them to be firmly planted and established in love. It would take being in this position to know and understand the love of Christ (verse 19).

If the love of Christ firmly dwells in us we will be equipped and able to love all mankind regardless of our differences. Of course, there will always be challenges due to different backgrounds, opinions, teachings, and the like. However, the love that is rooted and ground in us requires and equips us to love all mankind and realize the fact that we all have been equally created. The scriptures do not mention any account of God, the Ultimate Creator, the Author and Finisher of our faith, and the Great "I Am" creating humankind of separate and various levels. For God so loved "the world" (all mankind) that He gave His only begotten son as a ransom for all – not for some (John 3:16).

My prayer, as was the apostle Paul's, and I hope yours also, is that all believers understand, accept, and live this principle without fear or shame. If we are truly rooted and grounded in love (the God kind of love) we will treat others with dignity and respect, be concerned about each other's well-being, and desire God's best for all. We will love others as we love ourselves and will not be ashamed or fearful of living a rooted and grounded love life each and every day.

Finally, we should, as I mentioned earlier, pray the prayer that the apostle Paul prayed. We should pray that all born again believers pray for the body of Christ to be unified in love, thought, and deed. Let's get and remain rooted and grounded in love.

Why Do I Feel Down?

> Why am I discouraged? Why is my heart so sad? I will put my hope in God! I will praise him again— my Savior and my God! Now I am deeply discouraged, but I will remember you— (Psalms 42:5-6)

> Why am I discouraged? Why is my heart so sad? I will put my hope in God! I will praise him again— my Savior and my God (Psalms 42:11)

> Why am I discouraged? Why is my heart so sad? I will put my hope in God! I will praise him again— my Savior and my God! (Psalms 43:5)

Did you ever feel like everything was against you? Did you feel that life was so overwhelming that you just couldn't see your way out? Well, you're not alone. David felt this way. Yes, David – the man after God's own heart. David the psalmist, the poet, the king.

Why Do I Feel Down?

Brothers and sisters, there will be times in our lives when we feel all alone-literally. We may feel that God has left us. And like the Psalmist, we ask ourselves why? Why am I feeling lost, alone, depressed, down, hopeless? It is during these times that we, like the Psalmist did, must encourage ourselves in our God. It is during these moments when we must command our soul and everything on the inside of us to bless the Lord. (Psalm 103:1-2)

David is our example. He asked himself the question, why is my heart so sad? But then he said, even though my heart is sad, I will put my hope in God. I will praise him again. I will not be overtaken by my circumstances or what people say about me or how they treat me. Yes, it hurts. Yes, it bothers me. But I will put my hope in God. I will praise him again and again and again!

When you read through the entire verses of these Psalms 42-43, you'll see how overwhelming things were for David. He had a lot of questions about his current circumstances. Why has God forgotten me, why must I wander around in grief, why are my enemies oppressing me, why aren't things the way they used to be, why am I so discouraged, why is my heart so sad? Why?

Well, my brothers and sisters, sometimes we don't know why. We don't always understand the shifting in our lives. That is why we have to encourage ourselves in our God. That is why we must do what the Psalmist did. We must put our hope in God. We must praise Him again. We must remember what He did in previous times.

Though it takes a lot of effort, this is what we, the people of God must do to bring ourselves up and out. This becomes our testimony. This is our victory. If you're going through a season of loneliness, and emptiness, follow the Psalmist's lead. Tell yourself: "I will put my hope in God! I will praise him again – my Savior and my God"!

Feed Us and Fill Us

Then Jesus said unto them, "Verily, verily, I say unto you, Moses gave you not that bread from heaven; but my Father giveth you the true bread from heaven.

For the bread of God is he which cometh down from heaven, and giveth life unto the world."

Then said they unto him, Lord evermore give us this bread.

And Jesus said unto them, "I am the bread of life: he that cometh to me shall never hunger; and he that believeth on me shall never thirst" (John 6:32-35 KJV).

Father, feed us and fill us
with the true Bread from heaven.
Let us continuously eat
from your spiritual table.

Father, we long to be served by you -
the full course meal only You can give.
And please give an extra portion to
those of us who need it most.

Father, we know that every time we feast
from the blessings of Your Word,
we won't be able to digest it all,

BLESSINGS THROUGH THE WORD

but yet we will still want more.

Father, don't let us ever get enough
Of what You have for your children.
And every time we seek nourishment for our souls,
Feed us and fill us again.

SEE, HEAR AND UNDERSTAND!

Moses summoned all the Israelites and said to them, "You have seen with your own eyes everything the Lord did in the land of Egypt to Pharaoh and to all his servants and to his whole country— all the great tests of strength, the miraculous signs, and the amazing wonders. But to this day the Lord has not given you minds that understand, nor eyes that see, nor ears that hear! (Deuteronomy 29:2-4).

In this passage, Moses reminds them of what they had personally witnessed in the land of Egypt with Pharaoh and with his servants. But it's the last sentence that is most impactful. "But the Lord has not given you minds that understand, nor eyes that see, nor ears that hear!"

We tend to become dull to the miracles and victories that the Lord has brought us through. We fail to experience God's true blessings and presence because of our inability to fully understand what God has done for us. This scripture challenges us. Moses was at the end of his ministry. He had gone as far as he could go with the Israelites, and Joshua was prepared to take the baton and lead them into the promised land. This is Moses' last discourse with the Israelites.

Feed Us And Fill Us

He calls the people together to remind them of where they have come from, where they are going, and gives them a glimpse of their future. However, the people did not get it!

Jesus challenged His disciples in the same way. Jesus had fed more than 5000 and later fed more than 4000. When He was alone with His disciples, He told them to beware of the leaven of the Pharisees and Herod. They thought he was talking about physical bread and were arguing with each other because no one had brought any. "Don't you know or understand even yet? Are your hearts too hard to take it in? 'You have eyes—can't you see? You have ears—can't you hear?' Don't you remember anything at all?... "Don't you understand yet?" he asked them." (Mark 8:17-21)

Even the disciples "forgot" about the miracles in just a short time. Why? Because we are in the way. We often fail to focus on God's agenda for our lives. We spend more time and energy on what we want rather than on what God wants or even what He says. We act as if God doesn't know or have a plan. But if God is first as we say, and if we want to be obedient as we say, then we must have a continued commitment to understanding what we hear and see God do for us, and remember what He has already done for us! Then God will give us minds to understand, eyes that see, and ears that hear.

God wants us to have a mindset that we will fix our hearts on Him with the purpose to obey Him. We must decide to listen attentively, listen to obey, listen for understanding – in other words we will give earnest heed to what we hear. I want to encourage each of us to remember that our God does not change. He is the same as He was yesterday, He is the same today, and He will be the same always. It's up to us to see, hear and understand!

Celebrate Jesus

"And the angel said unto them, fear not: for, behold, I bring you good tidings of great joy, which shall be to all people. For unto you is born this day in the city of David, A Savior which is Christ the Lord. And this shall be a sign unto you; ye shall find the babe wrapped in swaddling clothes, lying in a manger. And suddenly there was with the angel a multitude of the heavenly host praising God, and saying, Glory to God in the highest, and on earth peace, good will toward men" (Luke 2:10-14 KJV).

Here we are, once again in the midst of the Christmas season. As has always been in the past (as far back as I can remember), several displays of colorful lights, trees (evergreen, real and artificial), decorations and sounds of happy music are all around. Sights and sounds of the season are in most neighborhoods and business districts.

But what is not as visible and what is not talked about as much is the real reason for the season. Christmas, in its true form, is the time we set aside to give a specially recognized celebration of the Almighty God bringing a Savior into the world. It's the annual time of the year we celebrate the birth of our Lord and Savior Jesus Christ.

The news of our Savior's birth was announced by the angel who said, "I bring you good tidings (news) of great joy." The good news was that a Savior for all people had been born. This truly was the greatest gift of all. Glory to God was proclaimed. Peace on earth was proclaimed. Good will toward men was proclaimed. Look at the impact this gift (the Savior) had and continues to have on the world.

My desire is that all would recognize, understand, and celebrate the true meaning of Christmas. My desire is that all people in every corner of the world would "celebrate Jesus." I am not saying Christmas should not be a time of giving gifts, being with family, and enjoying feasts. But, most important is to celebrate the ultimate gift God gave because He loved us and wanted to offer a Savior so that we (mankind) could be reunited into the fellowship we once had with Him. Simply stated, there has never been and never will be a Christmas without Christ.

I ask and challenge all who read or hear these words to remember the true reason for the season and commit to informing others of that reason and challenging them to spread the news as the angel did with those shepherds who watched over their sheep by night. Let's celebrate Jesus!

Do You Hear the Words Coming Out of Your Mouth?

I often marvel about the things I hear people say. Sometimes I hear the words, and ask myself, "Do they really hear what they are saying? It's unbelievable that at times, people really say things that don't make any sense, or say hurtful or disrespectful words, and feel like it doesn't matter. Then, at other times, I hear words of life that a person may speak. They are equally impactful, and bring about a different reaction in me. Those words are uplifting and encouraging – soothing even. Those words make me feel better about myself and my life-even when I'm going through a challenge.

Scripture has a lot and I mean a lot to say about the words that come out of our mouths. Proverbs 18:21 says this: "The tongue can bring death or life; those who love to talk will reap the consequences".

James writes these words about the tongue. "And among all the parts of the body, the tongue is a flame of fire. It is a whole world of wickedness, corrupting your entire body". It can set your whole life on fire, for it is set on fire by hell itself.

Blessings Through the Word

People can tame all kinds of animals, birds, reptiles, and fish, but no one can tame the tongue. It is restless and evil, full of deadly poison. Sometimes it praises our Lord and Father, and sometimes it curses those who have been made in the image of God. And so blessing and cursing come pouring out of the same mouth. Surely, my brothers and sisters, this is not right! (James 3:6-10)

What powerful words! One might think that these words may not apply to them because it's talking about an object. But no, my friend, these words are for you and me. Matthew recorded these words of Jesus "The words you say will either acquit you or condemn you." (Matthew 12:37)

So, the question is, what words are you speaking, and do you really hear the words coming out of your mouth? We as believers are exhorted in scripture to be mindful of the words we speak. Let's look at some of the adjectives that teach us what our words produce. They bring life or death. There are consequences for the words that we speak. The tongue is compared to fire. It can be destructive and corrupt our whole body and even our lives. The tongue cannot be tamed. It is restless, always looking for something to destroy. It can work positively or negatively. It can praise God and at the same time curse those who have been made in the image of God. The words we speak will either acquit us or condemn us when Christ comes back to judge us.

So, I say we have a choice to use our words for good or use them for evil. We can choose words of life or words of death. We should choose life. Let our words produce life. Let our words represent what is in our hearts. If our hearts

DoYouHearTheWordsComingOutOfYourMouth?

are pure, our words will be pure, and the pure in heart will see God. Let's make a conscious effort to pay attention to the words that are coming out of our mouths!

Grateful Expectation

> "Now to him who is able to do immeasurably more than all we ask or imagine, according to his power that is at work within us," (Ephesians 3:20, NIV); "However, as it is written: What no eye has seen, what no ear has heard, and what no human mind has conceived the things God has prepared for those who love him" (1 Corinthians 2:9, NIV).

We have entered our journey into a new year and a new decade – 2020. There is a lot of dialogue sharing and conversation about what is expected in this new year and how much success we (individually and collectively) will realize.

While thinking about this and in preparing for this devotional, the Lord reminded me of the prayer message the apostle Paul gave to the Ephesians in Chapter 3, verse 20: "Now unto him who is able to do immeasurably more than all we ask or imagine, according to the power that is at work within us." This tells me that my God is able to do much more than I can ask or think in connection with the

Grateful Expectation

power (Holy Spirit) at work in me. God filled me with His presence, His Spirit to be at work and accomplish things He wanted to perform in my life. Paul wanted the church at Ephesus to understand that principle and to live by and with it.

In 1 Corinthians 2:9, the apostle Paul tells the Corinthian church that we (as humans) really don't conceive, grasp or understand completely the things (good and great things) God has prepared for those who love Him. I love Him. Do you? If so, then we have great and wonderful things and times to look forward to.

But my main challenge in this writing is to remind you that we should not look and expect great things to begin at the start of a new year. We should live in "grateful expectation" at all times – each and every day. We do not serve a God Who shows up every January 1 to do something nice for us. We serve a God Who delights in doing good things for His children and shows up every day and all day.

I purpose to live in grateful expectation at all times and I encourage you to do the same. Never forget that God loved us from the foundation of the world and has pleasure in seeing us in a continual position of expectation of spiritual blessings first and then material blessings. He is a God Who supplies all our needs (Philippians 4:19). He will always do what He says and will never come short of His Word.

Let's all be careful not to reduce His love and care for us to a "one-day" prayer of expectation at the beginning of each year. Let's purpose to live in "grateful expectation" each and every day of our lives.

Don't Reject the Son

> If anyone hears what I am saying and does not observe it, I don't judge him; for I did not come to judge the world, but to save the world. Those who reject me and don't accept what I say have a judge — the word which I have spoken will judge them on the Last Day. For I have not spoken on my own initiative, but the Father who sent me has given me a command, namely, what to say and how to say it. And I know that his command is eternal life. So, what I say is simply what the Father has told me to say."
> (John 12:47-50)

When Jesus spoke these words, He had just entered Jerusalem and the people were praising Him and acknowledging that He was from God. They shouted, they sang, and even laid their garments on the ground in worship. Yet, Jesus did not get caught up in the moment. He did not want to miss the opportunity for a final warning to those who were present.

Don't Reject The Son

He pointed the people in the direction of His Father. From the beginning, Jesus plainly taught that He came to save the world (people), not condemn it (them) (John 3:17). Earlier in his ministry, Jesus taught that there was one greater who had power over life and death. (Mt. 10:28) Here, Jesus wanted to remind the people that not accepting His assignment to them would mean judgment from the Greater One.

Notice in this text that we are not judged if we hear and don't do what Christ says, but we are judged when we refuse to believe in Him. That is when the Father steps in. For to reject His Son is the same as rejecting Him, and rejection of His Son has eternal consequences. For Christ said that He simply obeyed the command of His Father by saying what His Father told Him to say.

This is a new year, and it is the time when many of us make new resolutions. We set new goals and start new projects. We even revisit some previous ones that we haven't accomplished and add those to our list. But brothers and sisters, let's not focus so much on us and forget about Christ. It is true some have never heard the gospel. But others have heard and dismissed Him choosing not to believe. Let us put Christ on our list. For our eternal hope rests on Jesus. He is the One who makes our relationship with the Father possible.

Jesus never took credit for anything He said or did. He always gave credit to His Father. The Father had a plan for us through His Son. We cannot skip over Jesus. We must believe in Him, who He said He was and what He said. He is our Savior, our redeemer, the Son of God, the Holy One of Israel, the Keeper of our souls, the Bright and Morning Star, Immanuel (God with us). He is the one speaks to us in these last days. (Hebrews 1:2). Let's not reject Him. If we do, we fall into the Father's judgment. Let's lift Him up. Let us receive all of the Father's blessings by believing in His Son. This is what brings pleasure to Him. He has glorified His Son. Let us also glorify Him.

God's Never-Ending Provision

2 Corinthians 9:10-15
10) "Now he that ministereth (serves, supplies) seed to the sower both minister (serves, supplies) bread for your food, and multiply your seed sown, and increase the fruits of your righteousness (the harvest of your prosperity): 11) Being enriched in everything to all bountifulness (liberality) which causes through us thanksgiving to God. 12) For the administration of this service not only supplieth the want (needs) of the saints, but is abundant (abounding, in full supply) also by many thanksgivings unto God; 13) While by the experiment (proof) of this ministration (ministry) they glorify God for your professed subjection (the obedience of your confession) into the gospel of Christ, and for your liberal distribution (sharing) unto them, and unto all men; 14) and by their prayer for you, which long after you (yearn for you)

the exceeding grace of God in you. 15) Thanks be unto God for His unspeakable (indescribable) gift. (KJV)"

Paul explains to the Corinthian church that it is God Who provides them with their seed or increase. He provides two parts of seed or increase. The first part is bread for their food. This refers to their daily substance, whether it is food, clothing, shelter, health, or finances. The second part is seed or increase for sowing (sharing or giving). It is the seed for sowing that God multiplies or increases. This multiplied or increased seed is always a result of the fruit of your righteousness (prosperity, which means favor, spiritual growth, health, wisdom, and other things in addition to money). When you do not sow the "sowing portion" of your seed but hold on to it (store it up) or use it for other than its intended purpose of sowing, there will be no increase of your righteousness (prosperity). Paul emphasizes that God gives to His children to first satisfy their daily need (Phil.4:19) and then to provide something for them to sow (give) to others. Those others include but are not limited to the local church, other ministries, the community, non-profit organizations, and individuals. What you sow should include your time, talent, and treasure (financial resources). When you sow accordingly, your seed becomes your investment upon which God promises a mighty and overwhelming return!

Paul states that when we receive and give liberally we give thanks to God because our giving not only supplies the needs of other saints but it also gives them a reason to give thanks to God for His provision. Paul adds that these

God's Never-ending Provision

receiving saints glorify God for what they (the Corinthians) say (profess or preach) and for what they freely give. They thank God that the Corinthians' talk and their walk match and complement each other. In their prayers, they yearn for God's continued blessing with His grace (unmerited favor) so that the Corinthians would continue to be obedient and sow to them because they realized that part of what they received would be used to sow into the lives of others.

Paul refers to God's seed as an indescribable gift. Words cannot properly define or explain God's giving. The lesson for us today is that God gives us seed (provision) for our daily bread (needs) and He gives us seed to "sow." The seed to sow is our time, talent, and treasure (financial resources). As we use the "sowing seed" to sow or invest, God promises to multiply our fruit (harvest) with continual prosperity (favor, spiritual growth, health, wisdom, finances).

If you are a child of God (in addition to being God's creation) He will provide you with all you need to sustain yourself and with abundance (full supply) to sow and bless others. God cannot and does not lie! Oh, what a blessing. To God be the glory!!

MAKE PRAYER YOUR PRACTICE

> However, he made a practice of withdrawing to remote places in order to pray. (Luke 5:16)
>
> One day soon afterward Jesus went up on a mountain to pray, and he prayed to God all night. (Luke 6:12)

One day Jesus told his disciples a story to show that they should always pray and never give up. "There was a judge in a certain city," he said, "who neither feared God nor cared about people. A widow of that city came to him repeatedly, saying, 'Give me justice in this dispute with my enemy.' The judge ignored her for a while, but finally he said to himself, 'I don't fear God or care about people, but this woman is driving me crazy. I'm going to see that she gets justice, because she is wearing me out with her constant requests!'"

Then the Lord said, "Learn a lesson from this unjust judge. Even he rendered a just decision in the end. So, don't you think God will surely give justice to his chosen people who cry out to him day and night? Will he keep putting them off I tell you, he will grant justice to them quickly! But when the Son of Man returns, how many will he find on the earth who have faith?" (Luke 18:1-8)

One of the things that I love most about Luke's account of the gospel is the attention that he gives to Jesus' prayer life. More than any of the other gospel accounts, Luke depicts the prayer life of Christ most vividly. Throughout his narrative, we are continually reminded that Jesus had an intimate relationship with His Father. Luke writes of so many examples of Christ's prayer life that you just can't miss it. I believe Luke also lived his life praying. He made prayer his practice as well.

The word practice is both a noun and a verb. When used as a noun it means repeated exercise in or performance of an activity or skill so as to acquire or maintain proficiency in it.

When used as a verb it means to perform (an activity) or exercise (skill) repeatedly or regularly in order to improve or maintain one's proficiency. To carry out or perform (a particular activity, method, or custom) habitually or regularly.

As believers, we ought to be doing both as we pray. We need to make praying our practice so that we will acquire or maintain proficiency in our prayer life. We also need to pray continually so that we develop and maintain a strong and effective prayer life.

Many believers throw out the word pray/prayer so lightly. Some don't pray at all because they feel there's a certain skill that's involved. Thus, they feel their prayers will not be answered. Others pray every now and then. But then there are those who actually make prayer their practice. These believers want to hear from God. They desire to be in God's presence. They long for God. David describes these believers in the book of Psalms, "As the deer longs for streams of water, so I long for you, O God. I thirst for God, the living God. When can I go and stand before him? (Psalm 42:1-2). These believers are not always asking God for something, but are seeking God for who He is. They love on God when they pray. They want to hear from Him.

They know that God hears and answers their prayers.

How would you evaluate your prayer life? Is prayer an exciting part of your relationship with your Father? Is prayer your practice? Is it your norm? If it isn't, meditate on the above scriptures as Luke takes us on the journey of how Christ lived. Ask Him like the early disciples to teach you how to pray. I promise you there is nothing compared to loving on our God in prayer.

Making prayer our practice is deeper than asking God to do something for us. It's time well spent in our spiritual, emotional, and physical development. It draws us closer to God. Prayer allows us to experience God's blessings and favor throughout our daily activities. Those who make prayer their practice quickly recognize when God is at work. They see things with a spiritual eye, and quickly thank Him.

They continue to strengthen their faith by making prayer the norm in their lives.

Today I challenge you that if you are not already making prayer your practice that you begin to participate more in praying, and develop an active prayer life. Once you do this, you will not be able to exist without spending time with your Father. Prayer will be your life line to God.

EVERYONE IS INCLUDED!

Our heavenly Father had a plan in mind for every single person from before the beginning of time. We often hear that God loves us. But sadly, it is not accepted that He loves all of us. There is not one person who exists that wasn't in God's plan. We need to think about that more often. Some people view the God of the scriptures as the God of the Jewish nation, and by default, those who are not Jewish have been included in the family of God. But that is not the picture God has revealed in scripture. It is true that God revealed Himself to the Jewish nation and desired that they would be His special people to represent Him in the earth. However, it was never His intent that He was exclusive only to them.

The prophet Isaiah wrote about God's inclusion for all nations when He said, " Also the sons of the foreigner who join themselves to the Lord to serve Him, and to love the name of the Lord, and to be His servants, to everyone who keeps from polluting the Sabbath and takes hold of My covenant, even them I will bring to My holy mountain and make them joyful in My house of prayer. Their burnt offerings and their sacrifices shall be accepted on My altar; for My house shall be called a house of prayer for all people". (Isaiah 56:6-7).

Everyone Is Included!

Paul, the apostle, spends much of his writing on the inclusiveness of God's plan for everyone. He calls it the mystery of God that was hidden in past ages. He explains it this way. "... by which, when you read it, you may understand my knowledge of the mystery of Christ, which in other generations was not made known to the sons of men, as it is now revealed to His holy apostles and prophets by the Spirit, how the Gentiles are fellow heirs, and fellow members, and partakers of the promise in Christ by the gospel. (Ephesians 3:4-6).

He further writes in the letter to the Galatians that God doesn't see people according to ethnicity, gender, nationality, or even class. All God sees is His creation whom He desires to be in fellowship with. There is neither Jew nor Greek, there is neither slave nor free, and there is neither male nor female, for you are all one in Christ Jesus. If you are Christ's, then you are Abraham's seed, and heirs according to the promise. (Galatians 3:28-29).

The good news of the gospel is that everyone is included! No one is left out for any reason! God loves all of His creation. Luke, the Gentile doctor who was the author of the Gospel of Luke and the Book of the Acts of the Apostles, wrote that when the angel came and announced the birth of Jesus to the shepherds, he said, "...For I bring you good news of great joy, which will be to all people. For unto you is born this day in the City of David, a Savior, who is Christ the Lord. (Luke 2:10-11).

This is the truth that God wants us to share with others. The door is open to all to accept Christ Jesus as the resurrected Son of God! This is good news! Our Father shows no partiality or favoritism. We are all the favorites of God. Let's get this truth down in our spirits. Let's share this good news with others that everyone is included!

Look for The Good

> "And we know that all things work together for good to them that love God, to them who are the called according to his purpose" (Romans 8:28 KJV).

Certainly Romans 8:28 is one of the most recognized and most quoted scriptures in the bible. It is recited to encourage, rescue, give strength, and assist believers while we go through trials and tests.

However, I want to bring some points to the forefront of our thinking and reckoning about reading and quoting this verse. First, the scripture contains the words "we know." Who are the we? Who are the people being talked about and talked to? Those people are the ones who love God and understand that God has called (petitioned) them to be included in His process of "showing up and showing out." We understand and accept the fact that God, in His infinite wisdom, has a definite purpose and plan in using us to show the world that He is able to do exceeding abundantly above all we ask or think (Ephesians 3:20).

Next, I want to emphasize that all things are "working and "working together for good." How often do we see our trials and tribulations all working together for our good? The question usually is "Something good is going to come out of this? You have got to be kidding!" God's Word does not lie. Some good thing(s) will result – maybe not when we expect it or want it, but something good will come on the scene.

Finally, if we know God is working things out for our good, we should expect the good. We should "look" for the good. I believe looking for the good will put and keep us in the right frame of mind as we go through our situations. Also, looking for the good will cause us to give thanks and rejoice even while we are going through. We won't concentrate on the problem(s) but will center our attention on the God Who loves us and has promised not leave us. We are reminded that we never walk alone.

What are you facing today? What test, trial, or tribulation is at your front door? What looks impossible to conquer? Look for the good in all of it and rest and trust God to deliver you out of all your adversities. The sooner you look for the good – the sooner you will find it.

GOD IS OUR REFUGE

In the past month, we have experienced something that we've never experienced in our lifetime. People are dying in numbers that we've never seen before because of the Coronavirus outbreak worldwide. We, in the United States, did not think it would impact us when the virus first took hold. We thought we lived too far away from danger. We thought we were safe. Our government officials told us that. So, we continued life as usual. Some people used scripture to give us the false hope that we were secure from the danger that was spreading quickly to other countries. And then it happened. The virus was in our country. We were now faced with this deadly virus that no one had a cure for. Little by little, our lives began to change. And now, we are in a state of limbo. No one knows what to do. No one has a cure causing many to fear for their lives. Thousands die in a day. Before it's all over, someone we know or know of, or someone who knows someone we know will either be infected and/or die from this virus.

Where is the hope for us? Who will listen to the clarion call that we need to get our lives in order? There have been numerous commentaries on what we should do to help stave off the numbers of infections and deaths, nonetheless, the fear intensifies. However, the true believers do not live in fear. They trust God as their refuge. They know He is our shelter and protection. He alone is our place of safety.

Psalm 91 is God's promise of protection. This scripture reminds us that God will protect us from deadly diseases. He will cover us with his feathers and shelter us with his wings. "If you make the Lord your refuge, if you make the Most High your shelter, no evil will conquer you; no plague will come near your home. For he will order his angels to protect you wherever you go" Psalm 91:9-11.

This scripture says WE must make the Lord our refuge (our protection, our shelter from trouble)! Then He will protect us and keep us safe. He further says in the following verses, "The Lord says, "I will rescue those who love me. I will protect those who trust in my name. When they call on me, I will answer; I will be with them in trouble. I will rescue and honor them. I will reward them with a long life and give them my salvation." Psalm 91:14-16.

Our source in everything is our Father. We must look to Him when things are well and when things are not so well. We must accept God's promises that He will take care of us and our households IF we put Him first. He's going to make Himself known. The psalmist wrote these words,

> "Be still, and know that I am God! I will be honored by every nation. I will be honored throughout the world." The Lord of Heaven's Armies is here among us; the God of Israel is our fortress. Psalms 46:10-11.

So, my brothers and sisters, if you come across anyone who needs some comfort through this crisis, let's direct their attention to our Father. Let us share the promises of God with them. We can offer them the best hope and cure for these trying times.

Remember Your Source

> "Now unto him that is able to do exceeding abundantly above all that we ask or think, according to the power that worketh in us, unto him be glory in the church by Christ Jesus throughout all ages, world without end. Amen." (Ephesians 3:20-21).

Here we are as a nation and the world dealing with a pandemic we did not ask for or properly plan for. The Coronavirus has infiltrated and changed the way we embrace our daily activities including dining out, visiting family and friends, and even traveling to places of employment and worship services. Panic has begun to govern the actions of many that include buying more than necessary from grocery stores, and in some instances performing violent acts.

Every day social media, television and radio contribute much (and most) of their time updating us of how many virus cases exist and the current death toll. It seems that the more some of us hear about it, the more we entertain fear. Many people seem to be confused, angry, and distant – so much so that they don't seem to be their normal selves.

Remember Your Source

I encourage and challenge you to turn/return to the Word of God to sustain and keep you in perfect peace during this difficult (and very real) time we are experiencing. The apostle Paul informed and reminded the church at Ephesus that they served a God Who is "able to do exceeding abundantly above all that we ask or think, according to the power that worketh in us." Our God is able to cover, protect, and guide us through every situation and circumstance we face. We (born again believers) must remember that the Omnipotent, Omnipresent, and Omniscient God we serve is our true Source. The economy, the political system, the workforce, nor any pandemic determines whether or not we continue to sustain and even strive during the most challenging times.

Remember your Source. He (the Holy Spirit) is with you at all times if you are a part of the royal family of God. No weapon formed against you shall prosper (Isaiah 54:17). He will keep you in perfect peace if you keep your mind focused on Him (Isaiah 26:3). Satan wants us to be distracted from God by all the negative things that are happening. Yes, these things are very real. But in times like these the world needs a Savior, Jesus Christ the Anointed One. If Jesus is the Author and Finisher of your faith then you have no reason to live a life of fear. God did not give us a spirit of fear, but the spirit of power, love, and a sound mind (2 Timothy 1:7).

Live a life of victory in the time of struggle. Live a life of peace in the time of uncertainty. Live a life of joy in the midst of sadness. Remember your Source.

Cast Your Care

> "Humble yourselves therefore under the mighty hand of God, that he may exalt you in due time: Casting all your care upon him; for he careth for you" (1 Peter 5:6-7).

How often have we heard or used the phrases "I don't care, who cares, or no one cares?" Probably more often than we think. Merriam - Webster Dictionary defines "care" as a suffering of mind or a disquieted state of mixed uncertainty, apprehension, and responsibility. When this level of concern and worry occurs our minds and emotions are not at ease.

In 1 Peter 5:6-7, Peter addressed his readers to be subject (responsible to and supporting of) one another. He challenged them to humble themselves under God's hand and to cast all their cares on Him because He cares for them. In mentioning "their cares" he is referring to their suffering of the mind or disquieted state of mixed uncertainty defined in the Merriam – Webster Dictionary. In mentioning "God's care" he is referring to God's love, attention, and provision.

CAST YOUR CARE

There are two particular points I want to emphasize here. The first is that the readers are encouraged to "humble" themselves in order that they may be exalted (verse 6). The second point is that the readers are encouraged to "cast, throw, get rid of" their heavyweight. What's so important about this? We must humble ourselves to the point of admitting that we are not strong enough to carry the stress and worries of this world. We must humble ourselves to the point of believing and accepting the fact that God is so concerned about our well-being that He does not want us to carry any unnecessary weight. He wants us to be free of every burden.

Surely we must trust God to the point of knowing that no problem is too difficult for Him to handle. As the saying goes, "from the top to the bottom, God can handle our problems." However, we must allow God to take control of what the apostle Peter instructed his readers to do – simply cast your care!

He can't (and won't) handle what we are not willing to let go. Hence, "let go and let God." Peter instructs his readers to "cast or throw off" their burdens and distractions. That implies to get rid of them with intense determination and force rather than just hoping God will work them out. Yes, be emphatic and deliberate about it.

Are you in a time of uncertainty, stress, discomfort or worry? I remind you of the apostle Peter instructed his readers to do - simply cast your care!

The Power of Intercessory Prayer

Oftentimes we don't realize the impact of our prayers when we pray on behalf of someone else or "intercede" for them. In Paul's letter to Timothy, he wrote "I urge you, first of all, to pray for all people. Ask God to help them; intercede on their behalf, and give thanks for them." (1 Timothy 2:1)

In both the Old and New Testaments prayers of intercession are prominent - even those that impact nature. Elijah prayed for it not to rain, and for three years there was no rain. James reminds us of this even as he encourages us to pray for one another. "Elijah was as human as we are, and yet when he prayed earnestly that no rain would fall, none fell for three and a half years! Then, when he prayed again, the sky sent down rain and the earth began to yield its crops" (James 5:17-18).

Moses was one who constantly interceded with God on behalf of the people. He interceded for his sister Miriam when she, along with Aaron spoke against him and she was struck with leprosy. (Numbers 12:13). He prayed on behalf of the people after they complained against God so much,

The Power Of Intercessory Prayer

He sent snakes into their camp that bit and killed many. (Numbers 21:6). Moses again interceded to God to preserve the life of the Israelites when the twelve spies returned from scouting out the land and ten scouts convinced the people there was no chance they could possess the land. Instead, they wanted to choose a leader and return to Egypt. They complained against God all night and so intensely that He was ready to destroy them. (Numbers 14:1-25).

It doesn't matter if we intercede on behalf of one or many, we must intercede. The early believers prayed for the release of Peter from jail. Scripture says that while he was in jail, the church prayed earnestly to God for his release. God released him and led him out of the prison by an angel. (Acts 12:5-11).

Abraham interceded for the city of Sodom for his nephew Lot. God was ready to destroy the city because of its constant wickedness and sin. Abraham did not want his nephew to be destroyed with the wicked. So, he interceded and asked to preserve the city if there were ten righteous people. God assured him that he would not destroy it if he could find ten righteous people. We know the ending. God destroyed the city, but he did preserve the life of Lot and his family by leading them out of the city by the hand of two angels. Scripture tells us "But God had listened to Abraham's request and kept Lot safe, removing him from the disaster that engulfed the cities on the plain" (Genesis 19:29).

What is my point in all this? Brothers and sisters, let's use the power that God gave us to change our circumstances and the lives of others. God hears the prayers of the righteous. "The heartfelt and persistent prayer of a righteous man (believer) can accomplish much [when put into action and made effective by God—it is dynamic and can have tremendous power" (James 5:16).

WALK WORTHY

"I therefore, the prisoner of the Lord, beseech you that ye walk worthy of the vocation wherewith ye are called" (Ephesians 4:1)

"That ye might walk worthy of the Lord unto all pleasing, being fruitful in every good work, and increasing in the knowledge of God" (Colossians 1:10)

"That ye would walk worthy of God, who hath called you unto his kingdom and glory" (1 Thessalonians 2:12)

Due to current challenges and issues facing the world, I am revisiting a topic I shared several months ago. These challenges and issues have become more aggressive during the past few months.

Every time I hear the phrase "walk worthy" I'm reminded to represent. To walk worthy of the Lord means to live a life that presents and represents Christ. It's a challenge of a few words but enormous responsibility.

Blessings Through the Word

In the books of Ephesians and Colossians, the apostle Paul writes from a Roman jail to the church at Ephesus, the Colossian Christians, and other churches of Asia Minor. In Thessalonians, he is writing from and during his long stay at Corinth. His message to all is emphatic and to the point: Continue to live and walk in a fashion that represents Christ. He had received reports that believers were "backsliding" to beliefs and practices they entertained before becoming Christians. As a result, their lifestyles (including worship) were looking more like walks of non-believers rather than walks of believers.

Paul's rebuke and challenge to the early Christian churches apply to current-day believers. We are encouraged to live our daily lives in ways that are pleasing to God and to be fruitful (effective) in all we do. When others see us and/or talk to us, they should see Christ. We have been called to live in ways that reflect God's goodness, compassion, and love. Our "worthy walk" is a daily vocation that requires dedication and commitment. We must be focused and prepared at all times to present Jesus to those who don't know Him as Lord and Savior.

Certainly, there are many distractions that can hinder us from allowing our light to shine so that others will see our good works and glorify our Father in heaven ("Matthew 5:16"). Hence, all the more reason to be reminded to stay focused and "on point" in our walk and lifestyle so that we will be victorious in winning souls to the kingdom. Remember, walking worthy is a vocation from God. He has called and equipped us (through the Holy Spirit) to live in ways that reflect holiness. No, it is not always easy. Yes, it can be done. We can do all things through Christ which strengthens us (Philippians 4:13). Walk worthy.

No Condemnation

> "For God so (greatly) loved and dearly prized the world, that He (even) gave His (one and) only begotten Son, so that whoever believes and trusts in Him (as Savior) shall not perish, but have eternal life. For God did not send the Son into the world to judge and condemn the world (that is, to initiate the final judgement of the world), but that the world might be saved through Him" (John 3:16-17, Amplified Bible).

Often, we see, hear, or read John 3:16. But verse 17 does not get as much attention. The verse specifically tells the reason (purpose) the Son came to earth in human form. It tells why He did not come and also why He did come. The thought to be understood is that God did not send Christ to "condemn" the world. The word "condemn" means to express complete disapproval of, typically in public; to censure or to sentence someone to a particular punishment, especially death (Oxford Languages Dictionary).

Once we understand why God sent His Son, then we can believe the "why" and accept the "work" that was completed by the Son's coming to the earth. When this process of understanding and acceptance is completed, the following applies: "Therefore there is now no condemnation (no guilty verdict, no punishment) for those who are in Christ Jesus (who believe in Him as personal Lord and Savior)" (Romans 8:1, Amplified Bible).

After accepting God's gift of salvation through His Only Begotten Son, the verdict or stain of condemnation no longer exists. There is no guilty verdict or punishment for those who have accepted Christ as their personal Lord and Savior. So, the purpose for Christ's coming was not to express disapproval or punish mankind. The latter part of verse 17 tells us the reason God did send His Son to the earth. That is, that the world might be saved through Him. God wanted the world saved because He (God) so loved the world (His creation). Verse 16 tells us that He "so loved" the world that he did not want the world to be without a "Savior."

Born again believers are in the class of blood-washed members of the family of God. We should not live in fear by thinking "am I good enough to be a member of the royal priesthood? Our names are written in the Lamb's Book of Life. God's purpose for sending His Son was fulfilled once Christ resurrected with all power. That finished work put the next move on mankind. If you have accepted that finished work through faith by confessing with your mouth and believing in your heart (Romans 10:9-10) you have been filed in the permanent category of "no condemnation."

Why have I shared this thought/teaching? It's because once we fully understand why Christ came and accept the reason for His coming, we can live a more productive spiritual life – a life without worry of whether we are good enough or will we "make it to heaven." We can live a life that's pleasing to God and serves as witness that all can be saved without fear of condemnation.

It Starts with the Mind

Have you ever wondered what the mind has to do with our relationship with our Father? What is the mind? How does the mind control our behavior and thoughts? Scripture teaches us the impact that our minds have on our ability and willingness to do or not do the will of God. Paul tells us in 2 Corinthians that if our minds are blind, we cannot believe the gospel. "If the Good News we preach is hidden behind a veil, it is hidden only from people who are perishing. Satan, who is the god of this world, has blinded the minds of those who don't believe. They are unable to see the glorious light of the Good News. They don't understand this message about the glory of Christ, who is the exact likeness of God." (2 Cor. 4:3-4)

Our minds are not just our brain, conscious thoughts, or our intellect. It is a thought process that starts with our spirit and is followed by our actions.

The New Testament uses 11 different words that are translated as "mind", but each means something a little different. For example, Matthew 22:37 reads "'You must love the Lord your God with all your heart, all your soul, and all your mind". The word mind in this verse is "dianoia" which means willpower or volition, yet it was simply translated "mind". The Old Testament gives us more clarity. Mind was translated from three Hebrew words, reins, kidneys, and spirit.

Reins control, lead, and direct action. A rider uses reins to guide a horse to make it do certain things. Our minds can guide us in a way to do the actions God wants us to do – obedience. Or just like some horses that are stubborn and willful, and pull and fight against the reigns to go another way, our minds can take us in the opposite direction away from God.

The second Hebrew word for mind is "kidneys". Our kidneys serve two major functions: to filter out and eliminate all the debris, waste and filth from our blood; and control and regulate the amount of blood flow into our bodies. So, it is with our minds. We use our minds to get rid of our negative thoughts – unforgiveness, resentments, etc., and we decide who will control or regulate our lives- the Holy Spirit or Satan.

The third Hebrew word for mind is "spirit". Our spirit is the core of our being and is separate from our brain. It has a continuing existence, unlike the brain. Our mind creates the thoughts of our hearts, and what leads to certain actions in our lives. However, there is an unregenerate spirit and a regenerate spirit. If we are born again, our spirit connects with the Spirit of God. We can now know God, and do His desired will. The unregenerate spirit has no power to connect with and thus goes against all that God desires. And as Paul says in his letter to the Corinthians, they do not have the ability nor willingness to do the will of God.

It Starts With The Mind

The choice is ours. Do we choose to let God lead our lives through the blood of His Son Jesus, or follow another spirit that offers us no hope and fulfillment for our lives? Do we choose to have the mind of Christ, or follow the god of this world? Do we choose to be led by the Spirit of God or by our natural inclinations? Do we choose to be transformed by the renewing of our minds so that we can do the acceptable and complete will of God; or do we choose to be conformed to the world? (Romans 12:2) Do we choose to put off the old man and its corruption; or do we renew the spirit of our mind and put on the new nature of Christ? (Ephesians 4:22-24)

My brothers and sisters, I encourage us to be more "mindful" of our relationship with Christ. Christ didn't die for us to live mediocre lives as we go about calling ourselves "Believers". He wants us to live a completely transformed life being connected with and led by His Spirit.

ENDURANCE FOR THE CROWN

> Dear brothers and sisters,[a] when troubles of any kind come your way, consider it an opportunity for great joy. For you know that when your faith is tested, your endurance has a chance to grow. So let it grow, for when your endurance is fully developed, you will be perfect and complete, needing nothing. (James 2-3)

One of the biggest misconceptions about our spiritual journey with Christ is that once we accept Him as Lord we will be problem-free. After all, Christ will give us victory in every situation, right? He will protect us from all evil and harm, right?

Something that I've learned over the years is that God is a God of balance. We are not incorrect in believing that God gives us victory. We are not incorrect in believing that He will protect us from all evil and harm. He does protect us and give us victory throughout this journey. But it is also true that God proves Himself to us through the struggles we face.

We must and will experience difficult times. We will have struggles of varying kinds. We will cry out to our Father when we feel that we are sinking. But those are the times when He proves Himself to us. But not only that, we must prove ourselves to God by the challenges we face.

James, says just that. He wrote his letter to the Jewish believers who had been scattered to different places probably because of the persecution in Jerusalem. James acknowledged the difficulties that they were facing and encouraged them to be strong and to keep their eyes on Christ.

He tells them that they should look at their struggles as an opportunity for great joy. Why? Because when our faith is tested we have an opportunity to grow endurance. If we aren't tested and challenged by our circumstances, we won't obtain the endurance that is needed for spiritual growth and maturity. He's telling believers that they are on their way to a destination, and there's something we must achieve in the process. We are looking ahead for something greater than what we see and experience now.

You see, endurance builds character. When we develop endurance, we are not swerved from our deliberate purpose and loyalty to our faith by even the greatest trials and sufferings. We persist in the face of all opposition. He makes this point in the following verses.

Dear brothers and sisters,[c] be patient as you wait for the Lord's return. Consider the farmers who patiently wait for the rains in the fall and in the spring. They eagerly look for the valuable harvest to ripen. You, too, must be patient. Take courage, for the coming of the Lord is near. (James 5:7-8).

For examples of patience in suffering, dear brothers and sisters, look at the prophets who spoke in the name of the Lord. We give great honor to those who endure under suffering. For instance, you know about Job, a man of great endurance. You can see how the Lord was kind to him at the end, for the Lord is full of tenderness and mercy. (James 5:10-11)

James is telling us in these verses that while we wait for the Lord's return, we must endure some struggles. We will have some pain. But these verses are not passive. We don't just sit back and do nothing until the Lord returns. We are building, growing, looking ahead. He first uses the farmer as an example. The farmer plants at certain times, looking for the rains to come so they will have the harvest they desire. They are working the land, doing what's necessary to prepare for the harvest. The rains come in the fall and spring which is needed for the harvest. But the harvest is the focus.

Then he reminds us of the suffering of the prophets. He says we admire them by giving them great honor because they did not give up when they faced their struggles. He even talked about Job never giving up. He said the Lord was kind to him in the end for He is full of tenderness and mercy.

So, my brothers and sisters, let's endure whatever comes our way. Let's purpose in our minds that we will never give up, or give in, or give out. Why? Because there is a crown waiting for us ahead.

Commanded Provision

1 Kings 17:1-16

Now Elijah the Tishbite, from Tishbe[a] in Gilead, said to Ahab, "As the Lord, the God of Israel, lives, whom I serve, there will be neither dew nor rain in the next few years except at my word." 2 Then the word of the Lord came to Elijah: 3 "Leave here, turn eastward and hide in the Kerith Ravine, east of the Jordan. 4 You will drink from the brook, and I have directed the ravens to supply you with food there." 5 So he did what the Lord had told him. He went to the Kerith Ravine, east of the Jordan, and stayed there. 6 The ravens brought him bread and meat in the morning and bread and meat in the evening, and he drank from the brook. 7 Some time later the brook dried up because there had been no rain in the land. 8 Then the word of the Lord came to him: 9 "Go at once to Zarephath in the region of Sidon and stay there. I have directed a widow there to supply you with food." 10 So he went to Zarephath. When he came to the town gate, a widow was there gathering sticks. He called to her and asked, "Would you bring me a little water in a jar so I may have a drink?" 11 As she was going to get it, he called, "And bring me, please, a piece of bread." 12 "As surely as the Lord your God lives," she replied, "I don't have any bread—only a handful of flour in a jar and a little olive oil in a jug. I am gathering a few sticks to take home and make a meal for myself and my son, that we may eat it—and die." 13 Elijah said to her, "Don't be afraid. Go home and do as you have said. But first make a small loaf of bread for me from what you have and bring it to me, and then make something for yourself and your son. 14 For this is what the Lord, the God of Israel, says: 'The jar of flour will not be used up and the jug of oil will not run dry until the day the Lord sends rain on the land.'" 15 She went away and did as Elijah had told her. So there was food every day for Elijah and for the woman and her family. 16 For the jar of flour was not used up and the jug of oil did not run dry, in keeping with the word of the Lord spoken by Elijah.

I want to share with you some insights about God's commanded provision. I don't want to just tell you that God will provide, but I want you to know and be absolutely sure that God cannot and will not provide for you unless He commands it. I want to inform you that God cannot and will not provide for and sustain you in difficult times unless He allows (permits) difficult times to come. God cannot and will not bring you through without testing your faith.

I also want you to know that God uses others to bless you and make things happen for you. I really want you to know that what you make happen for others (and particularly the man or woman of God) He, (God) makes happen for you.

So, we see in these verses that God orchestrated a drought, a difficult time of little, and then no rain. This meant no water to drink or food to eat. This drought lasted for three and a half years (see Luke 4:25). Verse four tells us God commanded the ravens to feed Elijah by the brook. Verse six tells us the ravens brought Elijah provision day and night - literally giving him enough food to sustain him day by day. When the brook dried up, God spoke to Elijah (verses 8-9) and told him to go to Zarephath because He had commanded a widow woman to sustain him. It was impossible for the widow woman to ignore or reject Elijah's request. She had no choice in the matter because God had commanded it. God used her as part of the process to provide for Elijah and sustain him.

Let's pay particular attention to the fact that on both occasions - at the brook and in Zarephath, Elijah had to go where God had provided food. God can and will lead you to a place of spiritual (and physical) provision and He will use people you would never think He would use to get the job done.

Notice in verse 15 that the bible says the widow woman did according to what the man of God said and as a result she and her house did eat for many days. The oil flowed and the meal multiplied in the midst and time of lack. Not only did God provide for Elijah. He also provided for the widow woman and her son. Not only did He do it for them but He has provided and will continue to provide for me. He has provided and will continue to provide for you.

Commanded Provision

It may look dark and grim right now. Maybe what was once your stockpile is now your "next to nothing." Maybe your brook has dried up. Maybe you have only a little bit of this and a little bit of that. Don't give up. Don't throw in the towel. It only takes a second for God to command provision and sustenance on your behalf. You don't know what raven God will use. You don't know what ram in the bush God has for you. You don't know what widow woman God will command in your favor. Keep your eyes and ears open. Go where God says to go. Do what God says to do. Say what God tells you to say. When He commands something, the wheels of reason roll off the scene and the wheels of miracles come into the picture. Your sack of lack becomes your box of good and plenty. When El Shaddai, the God of more than enough is in control, no good thing is withheld from you. Get up, live, breathe and walk in God's commanded provision.

The Right Way

"Trust in the Lord with all your heart and lean not to your own understanding" (Proverbs 3:5, NIV).

"There is a way that appears to be right, but in the end it leads to death" (Proverbs 14:12, NIV).

Recently, I was driving home from a business trip and decided to find my way home without any assistance. I knew that I had to head east to get to my town. After traveling for about half an hour I began to wonder why I had not seen any familiar landmarks. It was then that I decided to use a navigation system for help. I was correct in that I should be traveling east, but I had been going southeast instead of northeast. The navigation system put me in the right direction and allowed me to correct my mistake.

How true this is when it comes to our spiritual walk. Proverbs 3:5 instructs us to "trust in the Lord and not lean to our own understanding." Certainly there are times when we may feel we have the situation under control, we know what direction to take, or our past experiences give us an

The Right Way

advantage in solving our problems. However Proverbs 14:12 informs and teaches us differently. "There is a way that appears to be right, but in the end it leads to death." Why should we not rely on our own understanding? Because sometimes (often) the way we choose looks like the right and best way to go, but after the decision has been made we find that the decision has resulted in destruction and failure.

There is only one "right way." That way is given by God through the Holy Spirit to guide and lead us to righteousness, success, and avenues that are pleasing to Him. Other "ways" may look promising and rewarding but they will yield a completely different result. The "right way" may be the road less traveled but that does not mean the most popular decisions are the best decisions.

As I was reminded by the Holy Spirit as a result of my recent trip, we should always ask and seek God for understanding and direction. After all, He is the Omniscient (all knowing) One. He knows everything - there is nothing, absolutely nothing He does not know. I'm reminded and challenged to always choose the "right way." I'm reminding and challenging you to do the same.

What is Your Faith Producing?

> James 2:14-26
> What good is it, dear brothers and sisters, if you say you have faith but don't show it by your actions? Can that kind of faith save anyone? (verse 14)

So, you see, faith by itself isn't enough. Unless it produces good deeds, it is dead and useless. Now someone may argue, "Some people have faith; others have good deeds." But I say, "How can you show me your faith if you don't have good deeds? I will show you my faith by my good deeds." (verse 17-18)

Can't you see that faith without good deeds is useless? (verse 20)

So, you see, we are shown to be right with God by what we do, not by faith alone. (verse 24)

Just as the body is dead without breath,[i] so also faith is dead without good works. (verse 26)

What Is Your Faith Producing?

This letter from James is one of the earliest letters written to the church. James makes an appeal to the body of Christ that we should do more to reflect our responsibility with and to Christ by our actions.

In Acts 10:38, Luke writes, "And you know that God anointed Jesus of Nazareth with the Holy Spirit and with power. Then Jesus went around doing good and healing all who were oppressed by the devil, for God was with him".

Scripture encourages us to do good to all people when we have the opportunity, but especially to those in the family of faith. (Galatians 6:10)

James confronts the believers in this. He tells them that our saying we believe in Christ, but our actions not supporting what we say means nothing. What we say and what we do should be connected. You see faith, like love, is an action word. Our faith acts out in works of love. No matter the inconvenience or the challenge, we must still demonstrate our faith by doing good works. Otherwise, we have a dead faith – a nonworking unproductive faith.

This kind of faith does nothing at all to help anyone. Our righteousness, or right standing with God, not only comes from believing, it also comes from producing good works. We must understand that our salvation is not for us alone, but it is to show the love of God to others.

So, let us be mindful of this exhortation, and remember that faith without good works is dead, and we are shown to be right with God, by what we do, and not by faith alone.

We must ask ourselves the question, "What is my faith producing?"

Take Off the Veil

> "But whenever someone turns to the Lord, the veil is taken away. For the Lord is the Spirit, and wherever the Spirit of the Lord is, there is freedom. So all of us who have had that veil removed can see and reflect the glory of the Lord. And the Lord—who is the Spirit—makes us more and more like him as we are changed into his glorious image" (2 Cor 3:16-18)

There are times when believers in Christ endure the disappointment of loved ones who refuse to come to Him. We don't understand how they can't "see" how important and life-changing serving Christ is. It grieves our spirits when we extend so much of our energy to try to get them to understand the truth. We desire that they get to know Christ so they can be free from the power of darkness.

In Chapter 3 of 2 Corinthians, Paul addresses this issue by comparing the old way with the new way. Paul writes that even though the old way was glorious, it led to death. The new way is more glorious because it leads to our right standing with God! He qualifies this truth by saying that the old way was not glorious at all compared with the overwhelming glory of the new way. Therefore, the old way which was glorious to a certain degree was replaced by something more glorious that remains forever! (2 Cor 3:10-11)

He further compares these two glories by saying that this new glory brings a different response than the old glory. The old glory required that Moses put a veil over his face so the people of Israel would not see the glory, even though it was a fading glory. The people's minds were hardened. It brought fear to them to even see a glimpse of being in the presence of God. When people still focus on the law, the veil still covers their minds and hearts. The only way for the veil to be removed and for their hearts to be opened is by believing in Christ. Until one accepts Christ, the veil remains and they don't understand spiritual truths.

But when a person turns to the Lord, the veil is taken away. One can then see and reflect the glory of the Lord. And the difference between the fading glory, and this glory is that this glory makes us more and more like Him as we are changed into his glorious image. How magnificent is that!

This glory urges us to continue to win souls for Christ. "And as God's grace reaches more and more people, there will be great thanksgiving, and God will receive more and more glory. (2 Cor 4:15)

That is why we never give up. Though our bodies are dying, our spirits are being renewed every day. For our present troubles are small and won't last very long. Yet they produce for us a glory that vastly outweighs them and will last forever! (2 Cor 4:16-17)

With these promises in mind, we should continue to pray that the veil be taken away from the minds and hearts of those who currently are not able to "see" the truth.

How to Live an Effective Christian Life

> "But thou, O man of God, flee these things: and follow after righteousness, godliness, faith, love, patience, meekness. Fight the good fight of faith, lay hold on eternal life, whereunto thou art also called, and hast professed a good profession before many witnesses" (1 Timothy 6:11-12).

I have learned that you don't succeed by accident. You succeed on purpose. You are or become successful because you intend to do so. It never happens by accident or circumstance. You must prepare, put your mind to it, and put your plan in action. You will never possess what you are not willing to pursue.

This is the same message the "seasoned" apostle Paul gave to the young pastor, Timothy. He told him to fight the good fight of faith. As part of that message he told him that the success of Christian living depends on learning to do three things: flee, follow, and fight.

How To Live An Effective Christian Life

You must flee from things the devil initiates, distorts, and manipulates. One of the things (among many) named to flee or avoid is the love of money. It is classified as the root of all evil (see verse 10). You must follow after the things of God. These things include but are not limited to righteousness, godliness, faith, love, patience, and meekness. You must fight the good fight of faith. It is the only fight you are called to fight. You do it by believing in your heart and saying with your mouth. (Romans 10:10) That is how Christ defeated satan - with the Word of God.

Your two weapons for living a successful Christain life are the Word of God and the Name of Jesus. Psalm 119:105 tells us that God's Word is a lamp unto our feet and a light unto our path. The Word gives instruction for Godly living and guides and illuminates the way for a righteous lifestyle. Proverbs 18:10 tells us the name of Jesus is a strong tower - the righteous run to it and are safe.

Let's not think these words and directives applied only to those named in the scriptures. They apply to you, me, and all who want to please the Master by living an effective Christian life. We must always walk worthy of the vocation to which we have been called. it.

Are You In?

> Genesis 24:58
> "So, they called Rebekah. "Are you willing to go with this man?" they asked her. And she replied, "Yes, I will go."

One of my favorite accounts in scripture is the story of when Rebecca chose to be Isaac's wife. Here is a beautiful narrative about a woman's faith! In Genesis Chapter 24, the author shares with us the assignment that Abraham gave to his trusted servant to find a wife for his son Isaac. Sarah had passed away by this time, and Abraham knew that his time would come soon. He did not want Isaac to be alone. He discussed his concern with his most trusted servant and commissioned him to find a wife for his son. Abraham did not want his son to marry one of the local Canaanite women. He wanted a wife from among his relatives who lived a long way off. Under no circumstance was Isaac to go there to search for a wife or live among his relatives. He wanted his servant to go there to find a wife for Isaac and bring her back.

What if she didn't want to come? What if he couldn't find a wife? But Abraham reassured his servant that God would go before him to make sure he found a wife for his son. His servant agreed and left.

Upon arrival, he rested with his camels. He prayed for success that day. He didn't want to search for a long time. He asked the God of Abraham to choose Isaac's future wife and confirm it by two things. The first by giving him water at his request, and then offering to water his camels. Even before he had finished his prayer, Rebekah came with her water jug. He made his request for a drink. She quickly gave him water and offered to draw water for his camels. During his conversation with her, the servant found that she was a relative of Abraham! He gave her a few gifts. She went home to tell her family what had just happened to her while he waited by the well.

Her brother Laban came to the well and invited him to stay with them. The servant went to their house, explained his mission, stayed overnight, and was ready to leave the next morning. His mission was successful. He wanted to return quickly to his master. Her parents wanted her to stay for ten days before leaving. After all, this might be the last time they would ever see their daughter and sister again. But the servant was ready to go. They called Rebekah and asked her if she was willing to go with this man. She said yes, she would go.

She didn't say she would think it over. Her response was one of faith. "Yes, I will go." I often wondered what she thought was ahead of her. Why was she not afraid to go with this stranger? What if she didn't like Isaac? Maybe he wouldn't like her. Scripture doesn't give us any insight into

Blessings Through the Word

Rebekah's thoughts except that she was willing to go. She was in. No matter what the future held for her, she was in.

That's the question I have for you. "Are you in?" What are you willing to do for your God? How far will you go to be a part of God's divine plan? Do you need all your questions answered before you agree to make a decision?

Rebekah had what she needed to say yes. She said yes, and God blessed her! We'll talk more about this next month. But for now, ask yourself the question, "Am I in?"

Are You In? Part 2

Genesis 24:60-67; 25:19-24

What were Rebekah's thoughts as she traveled the long journey to meet her future husband? She no doubt had lots of questions for the servant. She was a curious young woman. She was also strong and courageous. I can imagine that Abraham's servant smiled on the way back with a knowing that he had found the perfect wife for Isaac.

Rebekah's family sent her away with this prophetic blessing. "Our sister, may you become the mother of many millions! May your descendants be strong and conquer the cities of their enemies." (Gen. 24:60) The blessing was a broad and specific one. She would bear many children. Her line would produce strong descendants and conquer their enemies. In other words, the blessing was for the future prosperity and success of her family. Wow! Little did they realize how this blessing would come to fruition.

But there was a challenge they faced. Once Rebekah and Isaac settled down together, she was not able to bear children. This circumstance grieved both of them. But the scripture tells us that Isaac pleaded to God that his

Blessings Through the Word

wife would have children. God heard his prayer. Rebekah became pregnant not with one child, but with two! She was going to have twins! A double blessing at one time! We can only imagine their joy. Scripture tells us that Isaac was 40 years old when he married Rebekah and 60 years old when she gave birth!

Rebekah's pregnancy, however, was tremendously difficult. The scripture tells us that the two children "struggled with each other in her womb". (Gen. 25:22) In other words, the children pushed against each other so intensely inside of her. It was so intense that she went to the Lord about it. "And the Lord told her, "The sons in your womb will become two nations. From the very beginning, the two nations will be rivals. One nation will be stronger than the other; and your older son will serve your younger son." (Gen. 25:23) So this was the reason there was such a fight between these children: She was carrying in her womb two rival nations! Wow! Again, imagine the thoughts that went through Rebekah's mind about this revelation!

Yet, Rebekah said yes to be a part of God's divine plan. She had no idea what was in her future, but she was willing to leave her family for the unknown. It was her yes that brought forth these two nations that have influenced the world! She was in! Jesus said these words: "If any of you wants to be my follower, you must give up your own way, take up your cross, and follow me." (Matthew 16:24)

Again, I ask the question, Are you in?

Sufficiency and Satisfaction

(Psalm 34:8-10, 107:8-9, Matthew 5:6)

There are a lot of discussions taking place these days about our nation's ills. Words like Covid, economics, recession, and racism are common in conversations of the day. There is a lot of ear in the hearts and minds of some people as they contemplate whether or not their income and/or savings will be sufficient to sustain them through these tough times. The economy experts continue to tell us that if our income and financial reserve are not sufficient we will not be able to live a satisfied life.

However, I want to remind you that complete sufficiency and satisfaction is found and realized only in the Almighty God and Jesus Christ Who is the Author and Finisher of our faith (Hebrews 12:2). The Lord has already blazed the trail and finished the course. Our daily success and continued sustainability can come only through Him.

Psalm 34:8-10 "Oh taste and see that the Lord is good: blessed is the man that trusteth in him (8). Oh fear (reverence and honor) the Lord, ye his saints: for there is no want (lack) to them that fear (reverence and honor) him (9). The young lions do lack, and suffer hunger: but they that seek the Lord shall not want (lack) any good thing (10).

The antidote to surviving in today's society and having sufficiency and satisfaction is simply trusting in the Lord. Notice verse 9 states that saints who trust in the Lord by showing honor and reverence will not be in lack - but will have what they need and desire. So the question is, "How do we honor and reverence God?" We honor and reverence God by being obedient to His way, His will, and His Word. If we walk in complete obedience to God we are guaranteed (according to God's Word) to live in sufficiency and satisfaction. Notice that verse 10 states..."they that seek (trust) the Lord shall not want (lack) any good thing." We must trust God with every aspect of our lives. We must live lives that are pleasing to Him and not lives that are pleasing to ourselves or to others. God is our Creator and all we do or say must be pleasing in His sight. That means we yield our lives to Him and trust that all outcomes will be outcomes of sufficiency and satisfaction.

> Psalm 107"8-9 - "Oh that men would praise the Lord for his goodness (loving kindness), and for his wonderful works to the children of men! (8). For he satisfieth the longing soul, and filleth the hungry soul with goodness" (9).

Sufficiency And Satisfaction

The true saints of God have a longing, an extreme desire to be in constant fellowship with Him and to totally trust Him. It is that extreme desire for fellowship and trust that God satisfies by filling us with His goodness (loving kindness). It is vitally important to understand that when God fills you with His goodness there is no room (in you) for insufficiency or dissatisfaction. Insufficiency or dissatisfaction cannot and will not exist in a vessel that is filled with God's goodness. There is no room for the "bad stuff" if a vessel is filled with the "good stuff." Now that's a revelation that will make you give God some praise!

Matthew 5:6 - "Blessed are they which do hunger and thirst after righteousness: for they shall be filled." You will "hunger and thirst after (for) righteousness" once you have realized you have void to fill and that void can only be filled by God. They shall be filled (Greek, chortazo) refers to a complete satisfaction. Remember, the psalmist's words in Psalm 107:9: "He satisfieth the longing soul, and filleth the hungry soul with righteousness."

In conclusion, if we always honor and reverence God by living in complete obedience to Him we will always experience sufficiency and satisfaction through His goodness and lovingkindness. We will never have to live in fear or lack because if we trust in God, He will keep us in perfect peace as we keep our minds stayed (focused) on Him (Isaiah 26:3).

Good News and Happiness

> "And the angel said unto them, fear not: for: behold, I bring you good tidings of great joy, which shall be to all people. For unto you is born this day in the city of David a savior; which is Christ the Lord" (Luke 2:10-11, KJV).

Today, the world is experiencing many extreme challenges: Covid 19, high unemployment, political party friction, economic and social distress, and systemic racism. Although these challenges are not evident in every country, they exist worldwide nonetheless.

In the midst of these "opportunities to overcome" I am reminded of the announcement that came to the shepherds as they watched over their sheep in the night-covered fields. "And the angel said unto them, fear not: for: behold, I bring you good tidings of great joy, which shall be to all people. For unto you is born this day in the city of David a savior; which is Christ the Lord."

Good News And Happiness

The Vocabulary.com Dictionary defines tidings as "an old-fashioned word for recent news. If someone says "I bring you good tidings!" it means they have information to share you will probably like. The same dictionary defines joy as the emotion of pleasure and happiness. Joy can also be the very thing that delights you. Also, joy in its spiritual meaning of expressing God's goodness is a deep-rooted, inspired happiness.

With the "not so good" news we have had during the past year, I want to remind you of the "good news" that was proclaimed many, many years ago. A Savior, Christ the Lord was born and His birth signaled the process of mankind's redemption. This birth was a result of God's love for the world (mankind) He created. He loved you and me so much that He gave His only begotten Son to us. If anyone accepts the gift God the Father gave through His Son the Savior, that individual inherits eternal life (John 3:16).

Therefore, the good news and happiness every Christmas season and every day of the year is that the gift of salvation is available to anyone who accepts it. Though we are currently in the midst of many trials and tests, setbacks and struggles, always remember to share the "good news and happiness."

Glorify God in Your Decisions

Recently, I (R.J. Lightsey) have been pondering why people make bad decisions. I tried to gain some ground in understanding why by thinking back to some of the bad decisions I have made over the years. I'll be completely honest and state that there were more bad decisions that came to mind than I care to think about. The common theme in all the bad decisions I had made is that I wanted to please and satisfy my own selfish desires. I did not seek God or His will in arriving at any of those regrettable outcomes. Therefore, even though I may have enjoyed the rides for a while, the end results were nothing less than disastrous.

Through self examination, I realized there is a process to making good decisions. Though the process is relatively short, it is a vital process to be followed in order to achieve positive outcomes. Of course the process has the ultimate goal of glorifying God in your decisions. If you keep that in mind, you will be more readily prepared to begin the process of making good decisions.

There are two (2) things I want to draw to your attention. First, God will allow you to fail, if you make bad decisions. In 1 Samuel 13:8-14 we see the failure of Saul because of the bad decision he made. As king, it was not his position to sacrifice burnt offerings. That task (responsibility) belonged to the priest, Samuel. Saul's decision was based on his self-will. He wanted to satisfy and draw attention to himself. In 1 Samuel 10:8 Saul was instructed by Samuel to wait until he (Samuel) arrived in Gilgal and he would offer the sacrifices for peace. Saul knew the instruction but he chose to ignore it. His bad decision cost him his kingship.

Second, God always has a door open to do what is right. In 1 Corinthians 10:13 we read, "There hath no temptation taken you but such as is common to man: but God is faithful, who will not suffer you to be tempted above that ye are able; but will with the temptation also make a way to escape, that ye may be able to bear it" (KJV). The point here is that God allows temptation to come your way. Satan tempts you, but God allows it. Since God has never and never will set you up to fail, He always, always makes or establishes a way for you to endure temptation without yielding to it. He always creates an exit door for you to go through and come out on the side of victory. He always provides a door that leads directly to a good decision. He won't make you go through that door but He will always show you the way. He does this because He wants you to know that there is no failure in Him and He will not set you up to fail.

To arrive at the right decision, you must understand why you (God's creation) exist. In Isaiah 43:5-7, God tells Israel, "Fear not: for I am with thee: I will bring thy seed from the east, and gather thee from the west; I will say to the north, give up; and to the south, keep not back: bring thy sons from far, and my daughters from the ends of the earth; even every one that is called by my name: for I have created him for my glory, I have formed him; yea, I have made him" (KJV). God says that everyone who is called by His name was created for His glory. As a child of the Most High King, your purpose is to glorify God in the earth realm and to reign with the authority, anointing, and favor He has given. That's why in 1 Corinthians 10:31 Paul instructs the church by saying, "Whether therefore ye eat, or drink, or whatsoever ye do, do all to the glory of God" (KJV). Half of the good decision-making process is understanding and practicing this principle.

An essential tool we have for making good decisions is the Word of God. In Luke 6:40, Jesus says, The disciple is not above his master: but every one that is perfect shall be as his master" (KJV). Let the Word show you God's commandments. Strive to be perfect (fully trained) by knowing and obeying God's Word - the written Word and Christ. If you want to be mature in your Christian walk, you must become Christ-like in your decision making. The only way to do this is to study the Word and become Christ-like. Philippians 2:5 tells us to possess the same mind as Christ Jesus. In Philippians 2:8 we read where Christ humbled Himself and was obedient.

Finally, you experience joy at the end of each and every good decision-making process because God will be glorified. If you delight yourself in Him and in pleasing Him, He will not withhold any good thing from you. God rewards those who diligently seek Him (Hebrews 11:6). Therefore, glorify God in your decisions!

CPSIA information can be obtained
at www.ICGtesting.com
Printed in the USA
LVHW080024121221
705948LV00014B/542